The Octavius of Minucius Felix

The Octavius of Minucius Felix

The Octavius of Minucius Felix

© Lighthouse Publishing 2018

All rights reserved. Without limiting the rights under copyright reserved above, no part of this publication may be reproduced, stored in a retrieval system, or transmitted, in any form or by any means (electronic, mechanical, photocopying, recording or otherwise), without the prior written permission of the copyright owner of this book.

Published by
Lighthouse Christian Publishing
SAN 257-4330
5531 Dufferin Drive
Savage, Minnesota, 55378
United States of America

www.lighthousechristianpublishing.com

The Octavius of Minucius Felix

Introductory Note.

[a.d. 210.] Though Tertullian is the founder of Latin Christianity, his contemporary Minucius Felix gives to Christian thought its earliest clothing in Latinity. The harshness and provincialism, with the *Græcisms*, if not the mere *Tertullianism*, of Tertullian, deprive him of high claims to be classed among Latin writers, as such; but in Minucius we find, at the very fountain-head of Christian Latinity, a disciple of Cicero and a precursor of Lactantius in the graces of style. The question of his originality is earnestly debated among moderns, as it was in some degree with the ancients. It turns upon the doubt as to his place with respect to Tertullian, whose *Apology* he seems to quote, or rather to abridge. But to me it seems evident that his argument reflects so strikingly that of Tertullian's *Testimony of the Soul*, coincident though it be with portions of the Apology, that we must make the date of the *Testimony* the pivot of our inquiry concerning Minucius. Now, Tertullian's *Apology* preceded the *Testimony*, and the latter preceded the essay on the *Flesh of Christ*. If the *Testimony* was quoted or employed by Minucius, therefore, he could not have written before a.d. 205; and the statement of Jerome is confirmed, which makes our author, and not Tertullian, the copyist. The modern discussion of the matter is an interesting literary controversy; not yet settled, perhaps, though the dip of the balance just now sustains my own impressions. But it is a very unimportant matter in itself, the primary place in Latin Christianity being necessarily adjudged to the commanding genius and fertile mind of Tertullian, while it is no discredit to assign to Minucius his proper but secondary credit, of showing, at the very outset of the literature of Western Christianity, that believers were not all illiterate men, nor destitute of polite erudition, and that the language of the Tusculan philosopher was not degraded by its new destination to the higher and holier service of the faith.

Like Tertullian, our author appears to have been a juris consult, at Rome, at some period of his history. Beautiful glimpses of his life and character and surroundings are gained from his own pages, and nearly all we know about him is to be found therein. So far, he is his own biographer. He probably continued a layman, and may have lived, as some suppose, till the middle of the third century.

It is not unimportant to note that we are still dealing with "the North-African school," and that Rome has nothing to do with the birth of Latin Christianity, as such. We have entered upon the third Christian century, and as yet the venerable apostolic see of the West has made no movement whatever towards the creation of a Latin literature among Christians. So far from being "the mother and mistress" of the churches, she is yet voiceless in Christendom; while Africa holds the mastery of Christian thought alike in her schools of Alexandria and Carthage. This, although it is our fourth volume, contains nothing to modify this fact; and yet the whole literature of early Christianity is contained in our series. Well said Æneas Sylvius, who afterwards became Pope Pius the Second, "Verily, before the Council of Nice, some regard there was unto the Bishops of Rome, *although but small.*" Holy men as most of them were, they are invisible and unfelt in the formation of Christian theology.

In our author's style and thought there is a charm and a fragrance which associate him, in my mind, with the pure spirit of "Mathetes," with whose *Epistle to Diognetus*, written nearly a hundred years before, it may be profitably compared. See also my prefatory remarks to Mathetes, and the reference to Bunsen which I have suffixed to the Notice of the Edinburgh editors.

In the Edinburgh series, Minucius comes into view after Cyprian, and not till the end of the thirteenth volume of that edition. It will gratify the scholar to find it here where it belongs, and not less to note that it has an index of its own, while in the Edinburgh edition its contents are indexed with those of Cyprian. Consequently, the joint index is rendered nearly worthless, and the injury and confusion resulting to the Contents of Cyprian are not inconsiderable.

Here follows the valuable Prefatory Notice of Dr. Wallis:

Minucius Felix is said by Jerome to have been an advocate at Rome prior to his conversion to Christianity. Very little else is known, however, of his history; and of his writings nothing with any certainty, except the following dialogue; although Jerome speaks of another tract as having, probably without reason, been ascribed to him.

The *Octavius*, which is here translated, is a supposed argument between the heathen Cæcilius and the Christian Octavius—the writer being requested to arbitrate between the disputants. The date of its composition is still a matter of keen dispute. The settlement of the point hinges upon the answer to the question—Whether, in the numerous passages which are strikingly similar, occurring in the *Apologeticus* and the *Octavius*, Tertullian borrowed from Minucius, or Minucius borrowed from Tertullian? If Minucius borrowed from Tertullian, he must have flourished in the commencement of the third century, as the *Apologeticus* was written about the year 198 a.d. If, on the other hand, Tertullian borrowed from Minucius, the *Octavius* was written probably about the year 166, and Minucius flourished in the reign of Marcus Aurelius. The later date was the one adopted by earlier critics, and the reasons for it are well given by Mr. Holden in his introduction. The earlier date was suggested by Rösler, maintained by Niebuhr, and elaborately defended by Muralto. An exhaustive exhibition of arguments in favor of the earlier date has been given by Adolf Ebert in his paper, *Tertullian's Verhältniss zu Minucius Felix*, Leipzig, 1868.

Of the literary character of the dialogue, it is sufficient to quote the testimony of the late Dean Milman: "Perhaps no late work, either Pagan or Christian, reminds us of the golden days of Latin prose so much as the *Octavius* of Minucius Felix."

In considering the claim of the dialogue to such praise as this, it must be borne in mind that the text as we have it is very uncertain, and often certainly corrupt; so that many passages seem to us confused, and some hopelessly obscure. Only one manuscript of the work has come down to us; which is now in the Imperial Library in Paris. It is beautifully written. Some editors have spoken of two other mss.; but it is now known that they were wrong. They supposed that the first edition was taken from a different ms. than the Codex Regius, and they were not aware that a codex in Brussels was merely a transcript of the one in Paris.

The *Octavius* appears in the ms. as the eighth book of Arnobius, and at first it was published as such. To Franciscus Balduinus (1560) is due the merit of having discovered the real author.

There are very many editions of the *Octavius*. Among the earlier, those of Gronovius (1709) and Davies (1712) are valuable. Among the later, Lindner (1760), Eduard de Muralto (1836), and Oehler (1847) may be mentioned. There is a very good English edition by the Rev. H. A. Holden, M.A., Cambridge, 1853. The most recent edition is that of Carl Halm, published under the auspices of the Imperial Academy of Letters in Vienna; Vindobonæ, 1867. Both Holden and Halm give new recensions of the Codex Regius.

The Octavius of Minucius Felix.

Chapter I.—Argument: Minucius Relates How Delightful to Him is the Recollection of the Things that Had Happened to Him with Octavius While He Was Associated with Him at Rome, and Especially of This Disputation.

When I consider and mentally review my remembrance of Octavius, my excellent and most faithful companion, the sweetness and charm of the man so clings to me, that I appear to myself in some sort as if I were returning to past times, and not merely recalling in my recollection things which have long since happened and gone by. Thus, in the degree in which the actual contemplation of him is withdrawn from my eyes, it is bound up in my heart and in my most intimate feelings. And it was not without reason that that remarkable and holy man, when he departed *this life*, left to me an unbounded regret for him, especially since he himself also glowed with such a love for me at all times, that, whether in matters of amusement or of business, he agreed with me in similarity of will, in either liking or disliking the same things. You would think that one mind had been shared between us two. Thus he alone was my confidant in my loves, my companion in my mistakes; and when, after the gloom had been dispersed, I emerged from the abyss of darkness into the light of wisdom and truth, he did not cast off his associate, but—what is more glorious still—he outstripped him. And thus, when my thoughts were traversing the entire period of our intimacy and friendship, the direction of my mind fixed itself chiefly on that discourse of his, wherein by very weighty arguments he converted Cæcilius, who was still cleaving to superstitious vanities, to the true religion.

Chapter II. —Argument: The Arrival of Octavius at Rome During the Time of the Public Holidays Was Very Agreeable to Minucius. Both of Them Were Desirous of Going to the Marine Baths of Ostia, with Cæcilius Associated with Them as a Companion of Minucius. On Their Way Together to the Sea, Cæcillus, Seeing an Image of Serapis, Raises His Hand to His Mouth, and Worships It.

For, for the sake of business and of visiting me, Octavius had hastened to Rome, having left his home, his wife, his children, and that which is most attractive in children, while yet their innocent years are attempting only half-uttered words, —a language all the sweeter for the very imperfection of the faltering tongue. And at this his arrival I cannot express in words with how great and with how impatient a joy I exulted, since the unexpected presence of a man so very dear to me greatly enhanced my gladness. Therefore, after one or two days, when the frequent enjoyment of our continual association had satisfied the craving of affection, and when we had ascertained by mutual narrative all that we were ignorant of about one another by reason of our separation, we agreed to go to that very pleasant city Ostia, that my body might have a soothing and appropriate remedy for drying its humors from the marine bathing, especially as the holidays of the courts at the vintage-time had released me from my cares. For at that time, after the summer days, the autumn season was tending to a milder temperature. And thus, when in the early morning we were going towards the sea along the shore (of the Tiber), that both the breathing air might gently refresh our limbs, and that the yielding sand might sink down under our easy footsteps with excessive pleasure; Cæcilius, observing an image of Serapis, raised his hand to his mouth, as is the custom of the superstitious common people, and pressed a kiss on it with his lips.

The Octavius

Chapter III. —Argument: Octavius, Displeased at the Act of This Superstitious Man, Sharply Reproaches Minucius, on the Ground that the Disgrace of This Wicked Deed is Reflected Not Less on Himself, as Cæcilius' Host, Than on Cæcilius.

Then Octavius said: "It is not the part of a good man, my brother Marcus, so to desert a man who abides by your side at home and abroad, in this blindness of vulgar ignorance, as that you should suffer him in such broad daylight as this to give himself up to stones, however they may be carved into images, anointed and crowned; since you know that the disgrace of this his error redounds in no less degree to your discredit than to his own." With this discourse of his we passed over the distance between the city and the sea, and we were now walking on the broad and open shore. There the gently rippling wave was smoothing the outside sands as if it would level them for a promenade; and as the sea is always restless, even when the winds are lulled, it came up on the shore, although not with waves crested and foaming, yet with waves crisped and curling. Just then we were excessively delighted at its vagaries, as on the very threshold of the water we were wetting the soles of our feet, and it now by turns approaching broke upon our feet, and now the wave retiring and retracing its course, sucked itself back into itself. And thus, slowly and quietly going along, we tracked the coast of the gently bending shore, beguiling the way with stories. These stories were related by Octavius, who was discoursing on navigation. But when we had occupied a sufficiently reasonable time of our walk with discourse, retracing the same way again, we trod the path with reverted footsteps. And when we came to that place where the little ships, drawn up on an oaken framework, were lying at rest supported above the (risk of) ground rot, we saw some boys eagerly gesticulating as they played at throwing shells into the sea. This play is: To choose a shell from the shore, rubbed and made smooth by the tossing of the waves; to take hold of the shell in a horizontal position with the fingers; to whirl it along sloping and as low down as possible upon the waves, that when thrown it may either skim the back of the wave, or may swim as it glides along with a smooth impulse, or may spring up as it cleaves the top of the waves, and rise as if lifted up with repeated springs. That boy claimed to be conqueror whose shell both went out furthest, and leaped up most frequently.

Chapter IV. —Argument: Cæcilius, Somewhat Grieved at This Kind of Rebuke Which for His Sake Minucius Had Had to Bear from Octavius, Begs to Argue with Octavius on the Truth of His Religion. Octavius with His Companion Consents, and Minucius Sits in the Middle Between Cæcilius and Octavius.

And thus, while we were all engaged in the enjoyment of this spectacle, Cæcilius was paying no attention, nor laughing at the contest; but silent, uneasy, standing apart, confessed by his countenance that he was grieving for I knew not what. To whom I said: "What is the matter? Wherefore do I not recognize, Cæcilius, your usual liveliness? and why do I seek vainly for that joyousness which is characteristic of your glances even in serious matters?" Then said he: "For some time our friend Octavius' speech has bitterly vexed and worried me, in which he, attacking you, reproached you with negligence, that he might under cover of that charge more seriously condemn me for ignorance. Therefore, I shall proceed further: the matter is now wholly and entirely between me and Octavius. If he is willing that I, a man of that form of opinion, should argue with him, he will now at once perceive that it is easier to hold an argument among his comrades, than to engage in close conflict after the manner of the philosophers. Let us be seated on those rocky barriers that are cast there for the protection of the baths, and that run far out into the deep, that we may be able both to rest after our journey, and to argue with more attention." And at his word we sat down, so that, by covering me on either side, they sheltered me in the midst of the three. Nor was this a matter of observance, or of rank, or of honor, because friendship always either receives or makes equals; but that, as an arbitrator, and being near to both, I might give my attention, and being in the middle, I might separate the two. Then Cæcilius began thus: —

Chapter V.—Argument: Cæcilius Begins His Argument First of All by Reminding Them that in Human Affairs All Things are Doubtful and Uncertain, and that Therefore, It is to Be Lamented that Christians, Who for the Most Part are Untrained and Illiterate Persons, Should Dare to Determine on Anything with Certainty Concerning the Chief of Things and the Divine Majesty: Hence He Argues that the World is Governed by No Providence, and Concludes that It is Better to Abide by the Received Forms of Religion.

"Although to you, Marcus my brother, the subject on which especially we are inquiring is not in doubt, inasmuch as, being carefully informed in both kinds of life, you have rejected the one and assented to the other, yet in the present case your mind must be so fashioned that you may hold the balance of a most just judge, nor lean with a disposition to one side (more than another), lest your decision may seem not to arise so much from our arguments, as to be originated from your own perceptions. Accordingly, If you sit in judgment on me, as a person who is new, and as one ignorant of either side, there is no difficulty in making plain that all things in human affairs are doubtful, uncertain, and unsettled, and that all things are rather probable than true. Wherefore it is the less wonderful that some, from the weariness of thoroughly investigating truth, should rashly succumb to any sort of opinion rather than persevere in exploring it with persistent diligence. And thus all men must be indignant, all men must feel pain, that certain persons—and these unskilled in learning, strangers to literature, without knowledge even of sordid arts—should dare to determine on any certainty concerning the nature at large, and the (divine) majesty, of which so many of the multitude of sects in all ages (still doubt), and philosophy itself deliberates still. Nor without reason; since the mediocrity of human intelligence is so far from (the capacity of) divine investigation, that neither is it given us to know, nor is it permitted to search, nor is it religious to ravish, the things that are supported in suspense in the heaven above us, nor the things which are deeply submerged below the earth; and we may rightly seem sufficiently happy and sufficiently prudent, if, according to that ancient oracle of the sage, we should know ourselves intimately. But even if we indulge in a senseless and useless labor, and wander away beyond the limits proper to our humility, and though, inclined towards the earth, we transcend with daring ambition heaven itself, and the very stars, let us at least not entangle this error with vain and fearful opinions. Let the seeds of all things have been in the beginning condensed by a nature combining them in itself—what God is the author here? Let the members of the whole world be by fortuitous concurrences united, digested, fashioned—what God is the contriver? Although fire may have lit up the stars; although (the lightness of) its own material may have suspended the heaven; although its own material may have established the earth by its weight; and although the sea may have flowed in from moisture, whence is this religion? Whence this fear? What is this superstition? Man, and every animal which is born, inspired with life, and nourished, is as a voluntary concretion of the elements, into which again man and every animal is divided, resolved, and dissipated. So all things flow back again into their source, and are turned again into themselves, without any artificer, or judge, or creator. Thus the seeds of fires, being gathered together, cause other suns, and

The Octavius

again others, always to shine forth. Thus the vapors of the earth, being exhaled, cause the mists always to grow, which being condensed and collected, cause the clouds to rise higher; and when they fall, cause the rains to flow, the winds to blow, the hail to rattle down; or when the clouds clash together, they cause the thunder to bellow, the lightnings to grow red, the thunderbolts to gleam forth. Therefore, they fall everywhere, they rush on the mountains, they strike the trees; without
any choice, they blast places sacred and profane; they smite mischievous men, and often, too, religious men. Why should I speak of tempests, various and uncertain, wherein the attack upon all things is tossed about without any order or discrimination? —in shipwrecks, that the fates of good and bad men are jumbled together, their deserts confounded? —in
conflagrations, that the destruction of innocent and guilty is united? —and when with the plague-taint of the sky a region is stained, that all perish without distinction? —and when the heat of war is raging, that it is the better men who generally fall? In peace also, not only is wickedness put on the same level with (the lot of) those who are better, but it is also regarded
in such esteem, that, in the case of many people, you know not whether their depravity is most to be detested, or their felicity to be desired. But if the world were governed by divine providence and by the authority of any deity, Phalaris and Dionysius would never have deserved to reign, Rutilius and Camillus would never have merited banishment, Socrates
would never have merited the poison. Behold the fruit-bearing trees, behold the harvest already white, the vintage, already dropping, is destroyed by the rain, is beaten down by the hail. Thus either an uncertain truth is hidden from us, and kept back; or, which is rather to be believed, in these various and wayward chances, fortune, unrestrained by laws, is ruling over us.

Chapter VI. —Argument: The Object of All Nations, and Especially of the Romans, in Worshipping Their Divinities, Has Been to Attain for Their Worship the Supreme Dominion Over the Whole Earth.

"Since, then, either fortune is certain or nature is uncertain, how much more reverential and better it is, as the high priests of truth, to receive the teaching of your ancestors, to cultivate the religions handed down to you, to adore the gods whom you were first trained by your parents to fear rather than to know with familiarity; not to assert an opinion concerning the deities, but to believe your forefathers, who, while the age was still untrained in the birth-times of the world itself, deserved to have gods either propitious to them, or as their kings. Thence, therefore, we see through all empires, and provinces, and cities, that each people has its national rites of worship, and adores its local gods: as the Eleusinians worship Ceres; the Phrygians, Mater; the Epidaurians, Æsculapius; the Chaldæans; Belus; the Syrians, Astarte; the Taurians, Diana; the Gauls, Mercurius; the Romans, all divinities. Thus their power and authority has occupied the circuit of the whole world: thus it has propagated its empire beyond the paths of the sun, and the bounds of the ocean itself; in that in their arms they practice a religious valor; in that they fortify their city with the religions of sacred rites, with chaste virgins, with many honors, and the names of priests; in that, when besieged and taken, all but the Capitol alone, they worship the gods which when angry any other people would have despised; and through the lines of the Gauls, marveling at the audacity of their superstition, they move unarmed with weapons, but armed with the worship of their religion; while in the city of an enemy, when taken while still in the fury of victory, they venerate the conquered deities; while in all directions they seek for the gods of the strangers, and make them their own; while they build altars even to unknown divinities, and to the Manes. Thus, in that they acknowledge the sacred institutions of all nations, they have also deserved their dominion. Hence the perpetual course of their veneration has continued, which is not weakened by the long lapse of time, but increased, because antiquity has been accustomed to attribute to ceremonies and temples so much of sanctity as it has ascribed of age.

Chapter VII. —Argument: That the Roman Auspices and Auguries Have Been Neglected with Ill Consequences, But Have Been Observed with Good Fortune.

"Nor yet by chance (for I would venture in the meantime even to take for granted *the point in debate*, and so to err on the safe side) have our ancestors succeeded in their undertakings either by the observance of auguries, or by consulting the entrails, or by the institution of sacred rites, or by the dedication of temples. Consider what is the record of books. You will at once discover that they have inaugurated the rites of all kinds of religions, either that the divine indulgence might be rewarded, or that the threatening anger might be averted, or that the wrath already swelling and raging might be appeased. Witness the Idæan mother, who at her arrival both approved the chastity of the matron, and delivered the city from the fear of the enemy. Witness the statues of the equestrian brothers, consecrated even as they had showed themselves on the lake, who, with horses breathless, foaming, and smoking, announced the victory over the Persian on the same day on which they had gained it. Witness the renewal of the games of the offended Jupiter, on account of the dream of a man of the people. And an acknowledged witness is the devotion of the Decii. Witness also Curtius, who filled up the opening of the profound chasm either with the mass, or with the glory of his knighthood. Moreover, more frequently than we wished have the auguries, when despised, borne witness to the presence of the gods: thus Allia is an unlucky name; thus the battle of Claudius and Junius is not a battle against the

Carthaginians, but a fatal shipwreck. Thus, that Thrasymenus might be both swollen and discolored with the blood of the Romans, Flaminius despised the auguries; and that we might again demand our standards from the Parthians, Crassus both deserved and scoffed at the imprecations of the terrible sisters. I omit the old stories, which are many, and I pass by the songs of the poets about the births, and the gifts, and the rewards of the gods. Moreover, I hasten over the fates predicted by the oracles, lest antiquity should appear to you excessively fabulous. Look at the temples and lanes of the gods by which the Roman city is both protected and armed: they are more august by the deities which are their inhabitants, who are present and constantly dwelling in them, than opulent by the ensigns and gifts of worship. Thence therefore the prophets, filled with the god, and mingled with him, collect futurity beforehand, give caution for dangers, medicine for diseases, hope for the afflicted, help to the wretched, solace to calamities, alleviation to labors. Even in our repose we see, we hear, we acknowledge the gods, whom in the day-time we impiously deny, refuse, and abjure.

Chapter VIII. —Argument: The Impious Temerity of Theodorus, Diagoras, and Protagoras is Not at All to Be Acquiesced In, Who Wished Either Altogether to
Get Rid of the Religion of the Gods, or at Least to Weaken It. But Infinitely Less to Be Endured is that Skulking and Light-Shunning People of the Christians,
Who Reject the Gods, and Who, Fearing to Die After Death, Do Not in the Meantime Fear to Die.

"Therefore, since the consent of all nations concerning the existence of the immortal gods remains established, although their nature or their origin remains uncertain, I suffer nobody swelling with such boldness, and with I know not what irreligious wisdom, who would strive to undermine or weaken this religion, so ancient, so useful, so wholesome, even

although he may be Theodorus of Cyrene, or one who is before him, Diagoras the Melian, to whom antiquity applied the surname of Atheist, —both of whom, by asseverating
that there were no gods, took away all the fear by which humanity is ruled, and all veneration absolutely; yet never will they prevail in this discipline of impiety, under the name and authority of their pretended philosophy. When the men of Athens both expelled Protagoras of Abdera, and in public assembly burnt his writings, because he disputed deliberately rather than profanely concerning the divinity, why is it not a thing to be lamented, that men (for you will bear with my making use pretty freely of the force of the plea that I
have undertaken)—that men, I say, of a reprobate, unlawful, and desperate faction, should rage against the gods? who, having gathered together from the lowest dregs the more unskilled, and women, credulous and, by the facility of their sex, yielding, establish a herd of a profane conspiracy, which is leagued together by nightly meetings, and solemn fasts and
inhuman meats—not by any sacred rite, but by that which requires expiation—a people skulking and shunning the light, silent in public, but garrulous in corners. They despise the temples as dead-houses, they reject the gods, they laugh at sacred things; wretched, they pity, if they are allowed, the priests; half naked themselves, they despise honors and purple robes. Oh, wondrous folly and incredible audacity! they despise present torments, although they fear those which are uncertain and future; and while they fear to die after death, they do not fear to die for the present: so does a deceitful hope soothe their fear with the solace of a revival.

Chapter IX. —Argument: The Religion of the Christians is Foolish, Inasmuch as They Worship a Crucified Man, and Even the Instrument Itself of His Punishment. They are Said to Worship the Head of an Ass, and Even the Nature of Their Father. They are Initiated by the Slaughter and the Blood of an Infant, and in Shameless Darkness They are All Mixed Up in an Uncertain Medley.

"And now, as wickeder things advance more fruitfully, and abandoned manners creep on day by day, those abominable shrines of an impious assembly are maturing themselves throughout the whole world. Assuredly this confederacy ought to be rooted out and execrated. They know one another by secret marks and insignia, and they love one another almost before they know one another. Everywhere also there is mingled among them a certain religion of lust, and they call one another promiscuously brothers and sisters, that even a not unusual debauchery may by the intervention of that sacred name become incestuous: it is thus that their vain and senseless superstition glories in crimes. Nor, concerning these things, would intelligent report speak of things so great and various, and requiring to be prefaced by an apology, unless truth were at the bottom of it. I hear that they adore the head of an ass, that basest of creatures, consecrated by I know not what silly persuasion, —a worthy and appropriate religion for such manners. Some say that they worship the *virilia* of their pontiff and priest, and adore the nature, as it were, of their common parent. I know not whether these things are false; certainly suspicion is applicable to secret and nocturnal rites; and he who explains their ceremonies by reference to a man punished by extreme suffering for his wickedness, and to the deadly wood of the cross, appropriates fitting altars for reprobate and wicked men, that they may worship what they deserve. Now the story about the initiation of young novices is as much to be detested as it is well known. An infant covered over with meal, that it may deceive the unwary, is

17

placed before him who is to be stained with their rites: this infant is slain by the young pupil, who has been urged on as if to harmless blows on the surface of the meal, with dark and secret wounds. Thirstily—O horror!—they lick up its blood; eagerly they divide its limbs. By this victim they are pledged together; with this consciousness of wickedness they are covenanted to mutual silence. Such sacred rites as these are more foul than any sacrileges. And of their banqueting it is well known all men speak of it everywhere; even the speech of our Cirtensian testifies to it. On a solemn day they assemble at the feast, with all their children, sisters, mothers, people of every sex and of every age. There, after much feasting, when the fellowship has grown warm, and the fervor of incestuous lust has grown hot with drunkenness, a dog that has been tied to the chandelier is provoked, by throwing a small piece of offal beyond the length of a line by which he is bound, to rush and spring; and thus the conscious light being overturned and extinguished in the shameless darkness, the connections of abominable lust involve them in the uncertainty of fate. Although not all in fact, yet in consciousness all are alike incestuous, since by the desire of all of them everything is sought for which can happen in the act of each individual.

Chapter X.—Argument: Whatever the Christians Worship, They Strive in Every Way to Conceal: They Have No Altars, No Temples, No Acknowledged Images. Their God, Like that of the Jews, is Said to Be One, Whom, Although They are Neither Able to See Nor to Show, They Think Nevertheless to Be Mischievous, Restless, and Unseasonably Inquisitive.

"I purposely pass over many things, for those that I have mentioned are already too many; and that all these, or the greater part of them, are true, the obscurity of their vile religion declares. For why do they endeavor with such pains to conceal and to cloak whatever they worship, since honorable things always rejoice in publicity, while crimes are kept secret? Why have they no altars, no temples, no acknowledged images? Why do they never speak openly, never congregate freely, unless for the reason that what they adore and conceal is either worthy of punishment, or something to be ashamed of? Moreover, whence or who is he, or where is the *one* God, solitary, desolate, whom no free people, no kingdoms, and not even Roman superstition, have known? The lonely and miserable nationality of the Jews worshipped one God, and one peculiar to itself; but they worshipped him openly, with temples, with altars, with victims, and with ceremonies; and he has so little force or power, that he is enslaved, with his own special nation, to the Roman deities. But the Christians, moreover, what wonders, what monstrosities do they feign!—that he who is their God, whom they can neither show nor behold, inquires diligently into the character of all, the acts of all, and, in fine, into their words and secret thoughts; that he runs about everywhere, and is everywhere present: they make him out to be troublesome, restless, even shamelessly inquisitive, since he is present at everything that is done, wanders in and out in all places, although, being occupied with the whole, he cannot give attention to particulars, nor can he be sufficient for the whole while he is busied with particulars. What! Because they threaten conflagration to the whole world, and to the universe itself, with all its stars, are they meditating its destruction?—as if either the eternal order constituted by the divine laws of nature would be disturbed, or the league of all the elements would be broken up, and the heavenly structure dissolved, and that fabric in which it is contained and bound together would be overthrown.

The Octavius

Chapter XI.—Argument: Besides Asserting the Future Conflagration of the Whole World, They Promise Afterwards the Resurrection of Our Bodies: and to the Righteous an Eternity of Most Blessed Life; To the Unrighteous, of Extreme Punishment.

"And, not content with this wild opinion, they add to it and associate with it old women's fables: they say that they will rise again after death, and ashes, and dust; and with I know not what confidence, they believe by turns in one another's lies: you would think that they had already lived again. It is a double evil and a twofold madness to denounce destruction to the heaven and the stars, which we leave just as we find them, and to promise eternity to ourselves, who are dead and extinct—who, as we are born, so also perish! It is for this cause, doubtless, also that they execrate our funeral piles, and condemn our burials by fire, as if everybody, even although it be withdrawn from the flames, were not, nevertheless, resolved into the earth by lapse of years and ages, and as if it mattered not whether wild beasts tore the body to pieces, or seas consumed it, or the ground covered it, or the flames carried it away; since for the carcasses every mode of sepulture is a penalty if they feel it; if they feel it not, in the very quickness of their destruction there is relief. Deceived by this error, they promise to themselves, as being good, a blessed and perpetual life after their death; to others, as being unrighteous, eternal punishment. Many things occur to me to say in addition, if the limits of my discourse did not hasten me. I have already shown, and take no more pains to prove, that they themselves are unrighteous; although, even if I should allow them to be righteous, yet your agreement also concurs with the opinions of many, that guilt and innocence are attributed by fate. For whatever we do, as some ascribe it to fate, so you refer it to God: thus it is according to your sect to believe that men will, not of their own accord, but as elected to will. Therefore you feign an iniquitous judge, who punishes in men, not their will, but their destiny. Yet I should be glad to be informed whether or no you rise again with bodies; and if so, with what bodies—whether with the same or with renewed bodies? Without a body? Then, as far as I know, there will neither be mind, nor soul, nor life. With the same body? But this has already been previously destroyed. With another body? Then it is a new man who is born, not the former one restored; and yet so long a time has passed away, innumerable ages have flowed by, and what single individual has returned from the dead either by the fate of Protesilaus, with permission to sojourn even for a few hours, or that we might believe it for an example? All such figments of an unhealthy belief, and vain sources of comfort, with which deceiving poets have trifled in the sweetness of their verse, have been disgracefully remolded by you, believing undoubtingly on your God.

Chapter XII. —Argument: Moreover, What Will Happen to the Christians Themselves After Death, May Be Anticipated from the Fact that Even Now They are Destitute of All Means, and are Afflicted with the Heaviest Calamities and Miseries.

"Neither do you at least take experience from things present, how the fruitless expectations of vain promise deceive you. Consider, wretched creatures, (from your lot) while you are yet living, what is threatening you after death. Behold, a portion of you—and, as you declare, the larger and better portion—are in want, are cold, are laboring in hard work and hunger; and God suffers it, He feigns; He either is not willing or not able to assist His people; and thus He is either weak or inequitable. Thou, who dreamest over a posthumous immortality, when thou art shaken by danger, when thou art consumed with fever, when thou art torn with pain, dost thou not then feel thy real condition? Dost thou not then acknowledge thy frailty? Poor wretch, art thou unwillingly convinced of thine infirmity, and wilt not confess it? But I omit matters that are common to all alike. Lo, for you there are threats, punishments, tortures, and crosses; and that no longer as objects of adoration, but as tortures to be undergone; fires also, which you both predict and fear. Where is that God who is able to help you when you come to life again, since he cannot help you while you are in this life? Do not the Romans, without any help from your God, govern, reign, have the enjoyment of the whole world, and have dominion over you? But you in the meantime, in suspense and anxiety, are abstaining from respectable enjoyments. You do not visit exhibitions; you have no concern in public displays; you reject the public banquets, and abhor the sacred contests; the meats previously tasted by, and the drinks made a libation of upon, the altars. Thus you stand in dread of the gods whom you deny. You do not wreath your heads with flowers; you do not grace your bodies with odors; you reserve unguents for funeral rites; you even refuse garlands to your sepulchers—pallid, trembling beings, worthy of the pity even of our gods! Thus, wretched as you are, you neither rise again, nor do you live in the meanwhile. Therefore, if you have any wisdom or modesty, cease from prying into the regions of the sky, and the destinies and secrets of the world: it is sufficient to look before your feet, especially for untaught, uncultivated, boorish, rustic people: they who have no capacity for understanding civil matters, are much more denied the ability to discuss divine.

Chapter XIII. —Argument: Cæcilius at Length Concludes that the New Religion is to Be Repudiated; And that We Must Not Rashly Pronounce Upon Doubtful Matters.

"However, if you have a desire to philosophize, let any one of you who is sufficiently great, imitate, if he can, Socrates the prince of wisdom. The answer of that man, whenever he was asked about celestial matters, is well known: *'What is above us is nothing to us.*' Well, therefore, did he deserve from the oracle the testimony of singular wisdom, which oracle he himself had a presentiment of, that he had been preferred to all men for the reason, not that he had discovered all things, but because he had learnt that he knew nothing. And thus the confession of ignorance is the height of wisdom. From this source flowed the safe doubting of Arcesilas, and long after of Carneades, and of very many of the Academics, in questions of the highest moment, in which species of philosophy the unlearned can do much with caution, and the learned can do gloriously. What! is not the hesitation of Simonides the lyric poet to be admired and followed by all? Which Simonides, when he was asked by Hiero the tyrant what, and what like he thought the gods to be, asked first of all for a day to deliberate; then postponed his reply for two days; and then, when pressed, he added only another; and finally, when the tyrant inquired into the causes of such a long delay, he replied that, the longer his research continued, the obscurer the truth became to

him. In my opinion also, things which are uncertain ought to be left as they are. Nor, while so many and so great men are deliberating, should we rashly and boldly give an opinion in another direction, lest either a childish superstition should be introduced, or all religion should be overthrown."

Chapter XIV. —Argument: With Something of the Pride of Self-Satisfaction, Cæcilius Urges Octavius to Reply to His Arguments; And Minucius with Modesty Answers Him, that He Must Not Exult at His Own by No Means Ordinary Eloquence, and at the Harmonious Variety of His Address.

Thus far Cæcilius; and smiling cheerfully (for the vehemence of his prolonged discourse had relaxed the ardor of his indignation), he added: "And what does Octavius venture to reply to this, a man of the race of Plautus, who, while he was chief among the millers, was still the lowest of philosophers?" "Restrain," said I, "your self-approval against him; for it is not worthy of you to exult at the harmony of your discourse, before the subject shall have been more fully argued on both sides; especially since your reasoning is striving after truth, not praise. And in however great a degree your discourse has delighted me by its subtile variety, yet I am very deeply moved, not concerning the present discussion, but concerning the entire kind of disputation—that for the most part the condition of truth should be changed according to the powers of discussion, and even the faculty of perspicuous eloquence. This is very well known to occur by reason of the facility of the hearers, who, being distracted by the allurement of words from attention to things, assent without distinction to everything that is said, and do not separate falsehood from truth; unaware that even in that which is incredible there is often truth, and in verisimilitude falsehood. Therefore the oftener they believe bold assertions, the more frequently they are convinced by those who are more clever, and thus are continually deceived by their temerity. They transfer the blame of the judge to the complaint of uncertainty; so that, everything being condemned, they would rather that all things should be left in suspense, than that they should decide about matters of doubt. Therefore, we must take care that we do not in such sort suffer from the hatred at once of all discourses, even as very many of the more simple kind are led to execration and hatred of men in general. For those who are carelessly credulous are deceived by those whom they thought worthy; and by and by, by a kindred error, they begin to suspect every one as wicked, and dread even those whom they might have regarded as excellent. Now therefore we are anxious—because in everything there may be argument on both sides; and on the one hand, the truth is for the most part obscure; and on the other side there is a marvelous subtlety, which sometimes by its abundance of words imitates the confidence of acknowledged proof—as carefully as possible to weigh each particular, that we may, while ready to applaud acuteness, yet elect, approve, and adopt those things which are right."

Chapter XV. —Argument: Cæcilius Retorts Upon Minucius, with Some Little Appearance of Being Hurt, that He is Foregoing the Office of a Religious Umpire, When He is Weakening the Force of His Argument. He Says that It Should Be Left to Octavius to Confute All that He Had Advanced.

"You are withdrawing," says Cæcilius, "from the office of a religious judge; for it is very unfair for you to weaken the force of my pleading by the interpolation of a very important argument, since Octavius has before him each thing that I have said, sound and unimpaired, if he can refute it." "What you are reproving," said I, "unless I am mistaken, I have brought forward for the common advantage, so that by a scrupulous examination we might weigh our decision, not by the pompous style of the eloquence, but by the solid character of the matter itself. Nor must our attention, as you complain, be any longer called away, but with absolute silence let us listen to the reply of our friend Januarius, who is now beckoning to us."

The Octavius

Chapter XVI. —Argument: Octavius Arranges His Reply, and Trusts that He Shall Be Able to Dilute the Bitterness of Reproach with the River of Truthful Words. He Proceeds to Weaken the Individual Arguments of Cæcilius. Nobody Need Complain that the Christians, Unlearned Though They May Be, Dispute About Heavenly Things Because It is Not the Authority of Him Who Argues, But the Truth of the Argument Itself, that Should Be Considered.

And thus Octavius began: "I will indeed speak as I shall be able to the best of my powers, and you must endeavor with me to dilute the very offensive strain of recriminations in the river of veracious words. Nor will I disguise in the outset, that the opinion of my friend Natalis has swayed to and fro in such an erratic, vague, and slippery manner, that we are compelled to doubt whether your information was confused, or whether it wavered backwards and forwards by mere mistake. For he varied at one time from believing the gods, at another time to being in a state of hesitation on the subject; so that the direct purpose of my reply was established with the greater uncertainty, by reason of the uncertainty of his proposition. But in my friend Natalis—I will not allow, I do not believe in, any chicanery—far from his simplicity is crafty trickery. What then? As he who knows not the right way, when as it happens one road is separated into many, because he knows not the way, remains in anxiety, and dares neither make choice of particular roads, nor try them all; so, if a man has no steadfast judgment of truth, even as his unbelieving suspicion is scattered, so his doubting opinion is unsettled. It is therefore no wonder if Cæcilius in the same way is cast about by the tide, and tossed hither and thither among things contrary and repugnant to one another; but that this may no longer be the case, I will convict and refute all that has been said, however diverse, confirming and approving the truth alone; and for the future he must neither doubt nor waver. And since my brother

broke out in such expressions as these, that he was grieved, that he was vexed, that he was indignant, that he regretted that illiterate, poor, unskilled people should dispute about heavenly things; let him know that all men are begotten alike, with a capacity and ability of reasoning and feeling, without preference of age, sex, or dignity. Nor do they obtain wisdom by fortune, but have it implanted by nature; moreover, the very philosophers themselves, or any others who have gone forth unto celebrity as discoverers of arts, before they attained an illustrious name by their mental skill, were esteemed plebeian, untaught, half-naked. Thus it is, that rich men, attached to their means, have been accustomed to gaze more upon their gold than upon heaven, while our sort of people, though poor, have both discovered wisdom, and have delivered their teaching to others; whence it appears that intelligence is not given to wealth, nor is gotten by study, but is begotten with the very formation of the mind. Therefore, it is nothing to be angry or to be grieved about, though any one should inquire, should think, should utter his thoughts about divine things; since what is wanted is not the authority of the arguer, but the truth of the argument itself: and even the more unskilled the discourse,
the more evident the reasoning, since it is not colored by the pomp of eloquence and grace; but as it is, it is sustained by the rule of right.

Chapter XVII. —Argument: Man Ought Indeed to Know Himself, But This Knowledge Cannot Be Attained by Him Unless He First of All Acknowledges the Entire
Scope of Things, and God Himself. And from the Constitution and Furniture of the World Itself, Every One Endowed with Reason Holds that It Was Established by God, and is Governed and Administered by Him.

"Neither do I refuse to admit what Cæcilius earnestly endeavored to maintain among the chief matters, that man ought to know himself, and to look around and see what he is, whence he is, why he is; whether collected together from the elements, or harmoniously formed of atoms, or rather made, formed, and animated by God. And it is this very thing which we cannot seek out and investigate without inquiry into the universe; since things are so coherent, so linked and associated together, that unless you diligently examine into the nature of divinity, you must be ignorant of that of humanity. Nor can you well perform your social duty unless you know that community of the world which is common to all, especially since in this respect we differ from the wild beasts, that while they are prone and tending to the earth, and are born to look upon nothing but their food, we, whose countenance is erect, whose look is turned towards heaven, as is our converse and reason, whereby we recognize, feel, and imitate God, have neither right nor reason to be ignorant of the celestial glory which forms itself into our eyes and senses. For it is as bad as the grossest sacrilege even, to seek on the ground for what you ought to find on high. Wherefore the rather, they who deny that this furniture of the whole world was perfected by the divine reason, and assert that it was heaped together by certain fragments casually adhering to each other, seem to me not to have either mind or sense, or, in fact, even sight itself. For what can possibly be so manifest, so confessed, and so evident, when you lift your eyes up to heaven, and look into the things which are below and around, than that there is some Deity of most excellent intelligence, by whom all nature is inspired, is moved, is nourished, is governed? Behold the heaven itself, how broadly it is expanded, how rapidly it is whirled around, either as it is distinguished in the night by its stars, or as it is lightened in the day by the sun, and you will know at once how the marvelous and divine balance of the Supreme Governor is engaged therein. Look also on the year, how it is made by the circuit of the sun; and look on the month, how the moon drives it around in her increase, her decline, and decay. What shall I say of the recurring changes of darkness and light; how there is thus provided for us an alternate restoration of labor and rest? Truly a more prolix discourse concerning the stars must be left to astronomers, whether as to how they govern the course of navigation, or bring on the season of ploughing or of reaping, each of which things not only needed a Supreme Artist and a perfect intelligence, nor only to create, to construct, and to arrange; but, moreover, they cannot be felt, perceived and understood without the highest intelligence and reason. What! when the order of the seasons and of the harvests is distinguished by steadfast variety, does it not attest its Author and Parent? As well the spring with its flowers, and the summer with its harvests, and the grateful maturity of autumn, and the wintry olive-gathering, are needful; and this order would easily be disturbed unless it were established by the highest intelligence. Now, how great is the providence needed, lest there should be nothing but winter to blast with its frost, or nothing but summer to scorch with its heat, to interpose the moderate temperature of autumn and spring, so that the unseen and harmless transitions of the year returning on its footsteps may glide by! Look attentively at the sea; it is bound by the law of its shore. Wherever there are trees, look how they are animated from the bowels of the earth! Consider the ocean; it ebbs and flows with alternate tides. Look at the fountains, how they gush in perpetual streams! Gaze on the rivers; they always roll on in regular courses. Why should I speak of the aptly ordered peaks of the mountains, the slopes of the hills, the expanses of the plains? Wherefore should I speak of the multiform protection provided by animated creatures against one another? —some armed with horns, some hedged with teeth, and shod with claws, and barbed with stings, or with freedom obtained by swiftness of feet, or by the capacity of soaring furnished by wings? The very beauty of our own figure especially confesses God to be its artificer: our upright stature, our uplooking countenance, our eyes placed at the top, as it were, for outlook; and all the rest of our senses as if arranged in a citadel.

Chapter XVIII. —Argument: Moreover, God Not Only Takes Care of the Universal World, But of Its Individual Parts. That by the Decree of the One God All Things are Governed, is Proved by the Illustration of Earthly Empires. But Although He, Being Infinite and Immense—And How Great He Is, is Known to Himself Alone—Cannot Either Be Seen or Named by Us, Yet His Glory is Beheld Most Clearly When the Use of All Titles is Laid Aside.

"It would be a long matter to go through particular instances. There is no member in man which is not calculated both for the sake of necessity and of ornament; and what is more wonderful still, all have the same form, but each has certain lineaments modified, and thus we are each found to be unlike to one another, while we all appear to be like in general. What is the reason of our being born? what means the desire of begetting? Is it not given by God, and that the breasts should become full of milk as the offspring grows to maturity, and that the tender progeny should grow up by the nourishment afforded by the abundance of the milky moisture? Neither does God have care alone for the universe as a whole, but also for its parts. Britain is deficient in sunshine, but it is refreshed by the warmth of the sea that flows around it. The river Nile tempers the dryness of Egypt; the Euphrates cultivates Mesopotamia; the river Indus makes up for the want of rains, and is said both to sow and to water the East. Now if, on entering any house, you should behold everything refined, well arranged, and adorned, assuredly you would believe that a master presided over it, and that he himself was much better than all those excellent things. So in this house of the world, when you look upon the heaven and the earth, its providence, its ordering, its law, believe that there is a Lord and Parent of the universe far more glorious than the stars themselves, and the parts of the whole world. Unless, perchance—since there is no doubt as to the existence of providence—you think that it is a subject of inquiry, whether the celestial kingdom is governed by the power of one or by the rule of many; and this matter itself does not involve much trouble in opening out, to one who considers earthly empires, for which the examples certainly are taken from heaven. When at any time was there an alliance in royal authority which either began with good faith or ceased without bloodshed? I pass over the Persians who gathered the augury for their chieftainship from the neighing of horses; and I do not quote that absolutely dead fable of the Theban brothers. The story about the twins (Romulus and Remus), in respect of the dominion of shepherds, and of a cottage, is very well known. The wars of the son-in-law and the father-in-law were scattered over the whole world; and the fortune of so great an empire could not receive two rulers. Look at other matters. The bees have one king; the flocks one leader; among the herds there is one ruler. Canst thou believe that in heaven there is a division of the supreme power, and that the whole authority of that true and divine empire is sundered, when it is manifest that God, the Parent of all, has neither beginning nor end—that He who gives birth to all gives perpetuity to Himself—that He who was before the world, was Himself to Himself instead of the world? He orders everything, whatever it is, by a word; arranges it by His wisdom; perfects it by His power. He can neither be seen—He is brighter than light; nor can be grasped—He is purer than touch; nor estimated; He is greater than all perceptions; infinite, immense, and how great is known to Himself alone. But our heart is too limited to understand Him, and therefore we are then worthily estimating Him when we say that He is beyond estimation. I will speak out in what manner I feel. He who thinks that he knows the magnitude of God, is diminishing it; he who desires not to lessen it, knows it not. Neither must you ask a name for God. God is His name. We have need of names when a multitude is to be separated into individuals by the special characteristics of names; to God, who is alone, the name God is the whole. If I were to call Him Father, you would judge Him to be earthly; if a King, you would suspect Him to be carnal; if a Lord, you will certainly understand Him to be mortal. Take away the additions of names, and you will behold His glory. What! is it not true that I have in this matter the consent of all men? I hear the common people, when they lift their hands to heaven, say nothing else but *Oh God*, and *God is great*, and *God is true*, and *if God shall permit*. Is this the natural discourse of the common people, or is it the prayer of a confessing Christian? And they who speak of Jupiter as the chief, are mistaken in the name indeed, but they are in agreement about the unity of the power.

Chapter XIX. —Argument: Moreover, the Poets Have Called Him the Parent of Gods and Men, the Creator of All Things, and Their Mind and Spirit. And, Besides, Even the More Excellent Philosophers Have Come Almost to the Same Conclusion as the Christians About the Unity of God.

"I hear the poets also announcing 'the One Father of gods and men;' and that such is the mind of mortal men as the Parent of all has appointed His day. What says the Mantuan Maro? Is it not even more plain, more apposite, more true? 'In the beginning,' says he, 'the spirit within nourishes, and the mind infused stirs the heaven and the earth,' and the other members 'of the world. Thence arises the race of men and of cattle,' and every other kind of animal. The same poet in another place calls that mind and spirit God. For these are his words: 'For that God pervades all the lands, and the tracts of the sea, and the profound heaven, from whom are men and cattle; from whom are rain and fire.' What else also is God announced to be by us, but mind, and reason, and spirit? Let us review, if it is agreeable, the teaching of philosophers. Although in varied kinds of discourse, yet in these matters you will find them concur and agree in this one opinion. I pass over those untrained and ancient ones who deserved to be called wise men for their sayings. Let Thales the Milesian be the first of all, for he first of all disputed about heavenly things. That same Thales the Milesian said that water was the beginning of things, but that God was that mind which from water formed all things. Ah! a higher and nobler account of water and spirit than to have ever been discovered by man. It was delivered to him by God. You see that the opinion of this original philosopher absolutely agrees with ours. Afterwards Anaximenes, and then Diogenes of Apollonia, decide that the air, infinite and unmeasured, is God. The agreement of these also as to the Divinity is like ours. But the description of Anaxagoras also is, that God is said to be the motion of an infinite mind; and the God of Pythagoras is the soul passing to and fro and intent, throughout the universal nature of things, from whom also the life of all animals is received. It is a known fact, that Xenophanes delivered that God was all infinity with a mind; and Antisthenes, that there are many gods of the people, but that one God of Nature was the chief of all; that Xeuxippus acknowledged as God a natural animal force whereby all things are governed. What says Democritus? Although the first discoverer of atoms, does not he especially speak of nature, which is the basis of forms, and intelligence, as God? Strato also himself says that God is nature. Moreover, Epicurus, the man who feigns either otiose gods or none at all, still places above all, Nature. Aristotle varies, but nevertheless assigns a unity of power: for at one time he says that Mind, at another the World, is God; at another time he sets God above the world. Heraclides of Pontus also ascribes, although in various ways, a divine mind to God. Theophrastus, and Zeno, and Chrysippus, and Cleanthes are indeed themselves of many forms of opinion but they are all brought back to the one fact of the unity of providence. For Cleanthes discoursed of God as of a mind, now of a soul, now of air, but for the most part of reason. Zeno, his master, will have the law of nature and of God, and sometimes the air, and sometimes reason, to be the beginning of all things. Moreover, by interpreting Juno to be the air, Jupiter the heaven, Neptune the sea, Vulcan to be fire, and in like manner by showing the other gods of the common people to be elements, he forcibly denounces and overcomes the public error. Chrysippus says almost the same. He believes that a divine force, a rational nature, and sometimes the world, and a fatal necessity, is God; and he follows the example of Zeno in his physiological interpretation of the poems of Hesiod, of Homer, and of Orpheus. Moreover, the teaching of Diogenes of Babylon is that of expounding and arguing that the birth of Jupiter, and the origin of Minerva, and this kind, are names for other things, not for gods. For Xenophon the Socratic says that the form of the true God cannot be seen, and therefore, ought not to be inquired after. Aristo the Stoic says that He cannot at all be comprehended. And both of them were sensible of the majesty of God, while they despaired of understanding Him. Plato has a clearer discourse about God, both in the matters themselves and in the names by which he expresses them; and his discourse would be altogether heavenly, if it were not occasionally fouled by a mixture of merely civil belief. Therefore, in his *Timæus* Plato's God is by His very name the parent of the world, the artificer of the soul, the fabricator of heavenly and earthly things, whom both to discover he declares is difficult, on account of His excessive and incredible power; and when you have discovered Him, impossible to speak of in public. The same almost are the opinions also which are ours. For we both know and speak of a God who is parent of all, and never speak of Him in public unless we are interrogated.

Chapter XX. —Argument: But If the World is Ruled by Providence and Governed by the Will of One God, an Ignorant Antipathy Ought Not to Carry Us Away into the Error of Agreement with It: Although Delighted with Its Own Fables, It Has Brought in Ridiculous Traditions. Nor is It Shown Less Plainly that the Worship of the Gods Has Always Been Silly and Impious, in that the Most Ancient of Men Have Venerated Their Kings, Their Illustrious Generals, and Inventors of Arts, on Account of Their Remarkable Deeds, No Otherwise Than as Gods.

"I have set forth the opinions almost of all the philosophers whose more illustrious glory it is to have pointed out that there is one God, although with many names; so that any one might think either that Christians are now philosophers, or that philosophers were then already Christians. But if the world is governed by providence, and directed by the will of one God, antiquity of unskilled people ought not, however delighted and charmed with its own fables, to carry us away into the mistake of a mutual agreement, when it is rebutted by the opinions of its own philosophers, who are supported by the authority both of reason and of antiquity. For our ancestors had such an easy faith in falsehoods, that they rashly believed even other monstrosities as marvelous wonders; a manifold Scylla, a Chimæra of many forms, and a Hydra rising again from its auspicious wounds, and Centaurs, horses entwined with their riders; and whatever Report was allowed to feign, they were entirely willing to listen to. Why should I refer to those old wives' fables, that men were changed from men into birds and beasts, and from men into trees and flowers? — which things, if they had happened at all, would happen again; and because they cannot happen now, therefore never happened at all. In like manner with respect to the gods too, our ancestors believed carelessly, credulously, with untrained simplicity;

while worshipping their kings religiously, desiring to look upon them when dead in outward forms, anxious to preserve their memories in statues, those things became sacred which had been taken up merely as consolations. Thereupon, and before the world was opened up by commerce, and before the nations confounded their rites and customs, each particular nation venerated its Founder, or illustrious Leader, or modest Queen braver than her sex, or the discoverer of any sort of faculty or art, as a citizen of worthy memory; and thus a reward was given to the deceased, and an example to those who were to follow.

Chapter XXI.—Argument: Octavius Attests the Fact that Men Were Adopted as Gods, by the Testimony of Euhemerus, Prodicus, Persæus, and Alexander the Great, Who Enumerate the Country, the Birthdays, and the Burial-Places of the Gods. Moreover He Sets Forth the Mournful Endings, Misfortunes, and Deaths of the Gods. And, in Addition, He Laughs at the Ridiculous and Disgusting Absurdities Which the Heathens Continually Allege About the Form and Appearance of Their Gods.

"Read the writings of the Stoics, or the writings of wise men, you will acknowledge these facts with me. On account of the merits of their virtue or of some gift, Euhemerus asserts that they were esteemed gods; and he enumerates their birthdays, their countries, their places of sepulture, and throughout various provinces points out these circumstances of the Dictæan Jupiter, and of the Delphic Apollo, and of the Pharian Isis, and of the Eleusinian Ceres. Prodicus speaks of men who were taken up among the gods, because they were helpful to the uses of men in their wanderings, by the discovery of new kinds of produce. Persæus philosophizes also to the same result; and he adds thereto, that the fruits discovered, and the discoverers of those same fruits, were called by the same names; as the passage of the comic writer runs, that Venus freezes without Bacchus and Ceres. Alexander the Great, the celebrated Macedonian, wrote in a remarkable document addressed to his mother, that under fear of his power there had been betrayed to him by the priest the secret of the gods having been men: to her he makes Vulcan the original of all, and then the race of Jupiter. And you behold the swallow and the cymbal of Isis, and the tomb of your Serapis or Osiris empty, with his limbs scattered about. Then consider the sacred rites themselves, and their very mysteries: you will find mournful deaths, misfortunes, and funerals, and the griefs and wailings of the miserable gods. Isis bewails, laments, and seeks after her lost son, with her Cynocephalus and her bald priests; and the wretched Isiacs beat their breasts, and imitate the grief of the most unhappy mother. By and by, when the little boy is found, Isis rejoices, and the priests exult, Cynocephalus the discoverer boasts, and they do not cease year by year either to lose what they find, or to find what they lose. Is it not ridiculous either to grieve for what you worship, or to worship that over which you grieve? Yet these were formerly Egyptian rites, and now are Roman ones. Ceres with her torches lighted, and surrounded with a serpent, with anxiety and solicitude tracks the footsteps of Proserpine, stolen away in her wandering, and corrupter. These are the Eleusinian mysteries. And what are the sacred rites of Jupiter? His nurse is a she-goat, and as an infant he is taken away from his greedy father, lest he should be devoured; and clanging uproar is dashed out of the cymbals of the Corybantes, lest the father should hear the infant's wailing. Cybele of Dindymus—I am ashamed to speak of it—who could not entice her adulterous lover, who unhappily was pleasing to her, to lewdness, because she herself, as being the mother of many gods, was ugly and old, mutilated him, doubtless that she might make a god of the eunuch. On account of this story, the Galli also worship her by the punishment of their emasculated body. Now certainly these things are not sacred rites, but tortures. What are the very forms and appearances (of the gods)? do they not argue the contemptible and disgraceful characters of your gods? Vulcan is a lame god, and crippled; Apollo, smooth-faced after so many ages; Æsculapius well bearded, notwithstanding that he is the son of the ever youthful Apollo; Neptune with sea-green eyes; Minerva with eyes bluish grey; Juno with ox-eyes; Mercury with winged feet; Pan with hoofed feet; Saturn with feet in fetters; Janus, indeed, wears two faces, as if that he might walk with looks turned back; Diana sometimes is a huntress, with her robe girded up high; and as the Ephesian she has many and fruitful breasts; and when exaggerated as Trivia, she is horrible with three heads and with many hands. What is your Jupiter himself? Now he is represented in a statue as beardless, now he is set up as bearded; and when he is called Hammon, he has horns; and when Capitolinus, then he wields the thunderbolts; and when Latiaris, he is sprinkled with gore; and when Feretrius, he is not approached; and not to mention any further the multitude of Jupiters, the monstrous appearances of Jupiter are as numerous as his names. Erigone was hanged from a noose, that as a virgin she might be glowing among the stars. The Castors die by turns, that they may live. Æsculapius, that he may rise into a god, is struck with a thunderbolt. Hercules, that he may put off humanity, is burnt up by the fires of OEta.

Chapter XXII.—Argument: Moreover, These Fables, Which at First Were Invented by Ignorant Men, Were Afterwards Celebrated by Others, and Chiefly by Poets, Who Did No Little Mischief to the Truth by Their Authority. By Fictions of This Kind, and by Falsehoods of a Yet More Attractive Nature, the Minds of Young People are Corrupted, and Thence They Miserably Grow Old in These Beliefs, Although, on the Other Hand, the Truth is Obvious to Them If They Will Only Seek After It.

"These fables and errors we both learn from ignorant parents, and, what is more serious still, we elaborate them in our very studies and instructions, especially in the verses of the poets, who as much as possible have prejudiced the truth by their authority. And for this reason Plato rightly expelled from the state which he had founded in his discourse, the illustrious Homer whom he had praised and crowned. For it was he especially who in the Trojan was allowed your gods, although he made jests of them, still to interfere in the affairs and doings of men: he brought them together in contest; he wounded Venus; he bound, wounded, and drove away Mars. He relates that Jupiter was set free by Briareus, so as not to be bound fast by the rest of the gods; and that he bewailed in showers of blood his son Sarpedon, because he could not snatch him from death; and that, enticed by the girdle of Venus, he lay more eagerly with his wife Juno than he was accustomed to do with his adulterous loves. Elsewhere Hercules threw out dung, and Apollo is feeding cattle for Admetus. Neptune, however, builds walls for Laomedon, and the unfortunate builder did not receive the wages for his work. Then Jupiter's thunderbolt is fabricated on the anvil with the arms of Æneas, although there were heaven, and thunderbolts, and lightnings long before Jupiter was born in Crete; and neither could the Cyclops

imitate, nor Jupiter himself help fearing, the flames of the real thunderbolt. Why should I speak of the detected adultery
of Mars and Venus, and of the violence of Jupiter against Ganymede,—a deed consecrated, (as you say,) in heaven? And all these things have been put forward with this view, that a certain authority might be gained for the vices of men. By these fictions, and such as these, and by lies of a more attractive kind, the minds of boys are corrupted; and with the same fables clinging to them, they grow up even to the strength of mature age; and, poor wretches, they grow old in the same beliefs, although the truth is plain, if they will only seek after it. For all the writers of antiquity, both Greek and Roman, have set forth that Saturn, the beginner of this race and multitude, was a man. Nepos knows this, and Cassius in his history; and Thallus and Diodorus speak the same thing. This Saturn then, driven from Crete, by the fear of his raging son, had come to Italy, and, received by the hospitality of Janus, taught those unskilled and rustic men many things,—as, being something of a Greek,
and polished,—to print letters for instance, to coin money, to make instruments. Therefore he preferred that his hiding-place, because he had been safely hidden (latent) there, should be called Latium; and he gave a city, from his own name, the name of Saturnia, and Janus, Janiculum, so that each of them left their names to the memory of posterity. Therefore it
was certainly a man that fled, certainly a man who was concealed, and the father of a man, and sprung from a man. He was declared, however, to be the son of earth or of heaven,
because among the Italians he was of unknown parents; as even to this day we call those who appear unexpectedly, sent from heaven, those who are ignoble and unknown, sons of the earth. His son Jupiter reigned at Crete after his father was driven out. There he died, there he had sons. To this day the cave of Jupiter is visited, and his sepulcher is shown, and he is convicted of being human by those very sacred rites of his.

Chapter XXIII.—Argument: Although the Heathens Acknowledge Their Kings to Be Mortal, Yet They Feign that They are Gods Even Against Their Own Will, Not Because of Their Belief in Their Divinity, But in Honor of the Power that They Have Exerted. Yet a True God Has Neither Rising Nor Setting. Thence Octavius Criticizes the Images and Shrines of the Gods.

"It is needless to go through each individual case, and to develop the entire series of that race, since in its first parents their mortality is proved, and must have flowed down into the rest by the very law of their succession, unless perhaps you fancy that they were gods after death; as by the perjury of Proculus, Romulus became a god; and by the good-will of the Mauritanians, Juba is a god; and other kings are divine who are consecrated, not in the faith of their divinity, but in honor of the power that they exercised. Moreover, this name is ascribed to those who are unwilling to bear it. They desire to persevere in their human condition. They fear that they may be made gods; although they are already old men, they do not wish it. Therefore neither are gods made from dead people, since a god cannot die; nor of people that are born, since everything which is born dies. But that is divine which has neither rising nor setting. For why, if they were born, are they not born in the present day also?—unless, perchance, Jupiter has already grown old, and child-bearing has failed in Juno, and Minerva has grown grey before she has borne children. Or has that process of generation ceased, for the reason that no assent is any longer yielded to fables of this kind? Besides, if the gods could create, they could not perish: we should have more gods than all men together; so that now, neither would the heaven contain them, nor the air receive them, nor the earth bear them. Whence it is manifest, that those were men whom we both read of as having been born, and known to have died. Who therefore doubts that the common people pray to and publicly worship the consecrated images of these men; in that the belief and mind of the ignorant is deceived by the perfection of art, is blinded by the glitter of gold, is dimmed with the shining of silver and the whiteness of ivory? But if any one were to present to his mind with what instruments and with what machinery every image is formed, he would blush that he had feared matter, treated after his fancy by the artificer to make a god. For a god of wood, a portion perhaps of a pile, or of an unlucky log, is hung up, is cut, is hewn, is planed; and a god of brass or of silver, often from an impure vessel, as was done by the Egyptian king, is fused, is beaten with hammers and forged on anvils; and the god of stone is cut, is sculptured, and is polished by some abandoned man, nor feels the injury done to him in his nativity, any more than afterwards it feels the worship flowing from your veneration; unless perhaps the stone, or the wood, or the silver is not yet a god. When, therefore, does the god begin his existence? Lo, it is melted, it is wrought, it is sculptured—it is not yet a god; lo, it is soldered, it is built together—it is set up, and even yet it is not a god; lo, it is adorned, it is consecrated, it is prayed to—then at length it is a god, when man has chosen it to be so, and for the purpose has dedicated it.

Chapter XXIV.—Argument: He Briefly Shows, Moreover, What Ridiculous, Obscene, and Cruel Rites Were Observed in Celebrating the Mysteries of Certain Gods.

"How much more truly do dumb animals naturally judge concerning your gods? Mice, swallows, kites, know that they have no feeling: they gnaw them, they trample on them, they sit upon them; and unless you drive them off, they build their nests in the very mouth of your god. Spiders, indeed, weave their webs over his face, and suspend their threads from his very head. You wipe, cleanse, scrape, and you protect and fear those whom you make; while not one of you thinks that he ought to know God before he worships Him; desiring without consideration to obey their ancestors, choosing rather to become an addition to the error of others, than to trust themselves; in that they know nothing of what they fear.

Thus avarice has been consecrated in gold and silver; thus the form of empty statues has been established; thus has arisen Roman superstition. And if you reconsider the rites of these gods, how many things are laughable, and how many also pitiable! Naked people run about in the raw winter; some walk bonneted, and carry around old bucklers, or beat drums,

or lead their gods a-begging through the streets. Some fanes it is permitted to approach once a year, some it is forbidden to visit at all. There is one place where a man may not go, and there are some that are sacred from women: it is a crime needing atonement for a slave even to be present at some ceremonies. Some sacred places are crowned by a woman having one husband, some by a woman with many; and she who can reckon up most adulteries is sought after with most religious zeal. What! would not a man who makes libations of his own blood, and supplicates (his god) by his own wounds, be better if he were altogether profane, than religious in such a way is this? And he whose shameful parts are cut off, how greatly does he wrong God in seeking to propitiate Him in this manner! since, if God wished for eunuchs, He could bring them as such into existence, and would not make them so afterwards. Who does not perceive that people of unsound mind, and of weak and degraded apprehension, are foolish in these things, and that the very multitude of those who err affords to each of them mutual patronage? Here the defense of the general madness is the multitude of the mad people.

The Octavius

Chapter XXV.—Argument: Then He Shows that Cæcilius Had Been Wrong in Asserting that the Romans Had Gained Their Power Over the Whole World by Means of the Due Observance of Superstitions of This Kind. Rather the Romans in Their Origin Were Collected by Crime, and Grew by the Terrors of Their Ferocity. And Therefore the Romans Were Not So Great Because They Were Religious, But Because They Were Sacrilegious with Impunity.

"Nevertheless, you will say that that very superstition itself gave, increased, and established their empire for the Romans, since they prevailed not so much by their valor as by their religion and piety. Doubtless the illustrious and noble justice of the Romans had its beginning from the very cradle of the growing empire. Did they not in their origin, when gathered together and fortified by crime, grow by the terror of their own fierceness? For the first people were assembled together as to an asylum. Abandoned people, profligate, incestuous, assassins, traitors, had flocked together; and in order that Romulus himself, their commander and governor, might excel his people in guilt, he committed fratricide. These are the first auspices of the religious state! By and by they carried off, violated, and ruined foreign virgins, already betrothed, already destined for husbands, and even some young women from their marriage vows—a thing unexampled—and then engaged in war with their parents, that is, with their fathers-in-law, and shed the blood of their kindred. What more irreligious, what more audacious, what could be safer than the very confidence of crime? Now, to drive their neighbors from the land, to overthrow the nearest cities, with their temples and altars, to drive them into captivity, to grow up by the losses of others and by their own crimes, is the course of training common to the rest of the kings and the latest leaders with Romulus. Thus, whatever the Romans hold, cultivate, possess, is the spoil of their audacity. All their temples are built from the spoils of violence, that is, from the ruins of cities, from the spoils of the gods, from the murders of priests. This is to insult and scorn, to yield to conquered religions, to adore them when captive, after having vanquished them. For to adore what you have taken by force, is to consecrate sacrilege, not divinities.

As often, therefore, as the Romans triumphed, so often they were polluted; and as many trophies as they gained from the nations, so many spoils did they take from the gods. Therefore the Romans were not so great because they were religious, but because they were sacrilegious with impunity. For neither were they able in the wars themselves to have the help of the gods against whom they took up arms; and they began to worship those when they were triumphed over, whom they had previously challenged. But what avail such gods as those on behalf of the Romans, who had had no power on behalf of their own worshippers against the Roman arms? For we know the indigenous gods of the Romans—Romulus, Picus, Tiberinus, and Consus, and Pilumnus, and Picumnus. Tatius both discovered and worshipped Cloacina; Hostilius, Fear and Pallor. Subsequently Fever was dedicated by I know not whom: such was the superstition that nourished that city,— diseases and ill states of health. Assuredly also Acca Laurentia, and Flora, infamous harlots, must be reckoned among the diseases and the gods of the Romans. Such as these doubtless enlarged the dominion of the Romans, in opposition to others who were worshipped by the nations: for against their own people neither did the Thracian Mars, nor the Cretan Jupiter, nor Juno, now of Argos, now of Samos, now of Carthage, nor Diana of Tauris, nor the Idæan Mother, nor those Egyptian—not deities, but monstrosities—assist them; unless perchance among the Romans the chastity of virgins was greater, or the religion of the priests more holy: though absolutely among very many of the virgins unchastity was punished, in that they, doubtless without the knowledge of Vesta, had intercourse too carelessly with men; and for the rest their impunity arose not from the better protection of their

The Octavius

chastity, but from the better fortune of their immodesty. And where are adulteries better arranged by the priests than among the very altars and shrines? where are more pandering debated, or more acts of violence concerted? Finally, burning lust is more frequently gratified in the little chambers of the keepers of the temple, than in the brothels themselves. And still, long before the Romans, by the ordering of God, the Assyrians held dominion, the Medes, the Persians, the Greeks also, and the Egyptians, although they had not any Pontiffs, nor Arvales, nor Salii, nor Vestals, nor Augurs, nor chickens shut up in a coop, by whose feeding or abstinence the highest concerns of the state were to be governed.

Chapter XXVI.—Argument: The Weapon that Cæcilius Had Slightly Brandished Against Him, Taken from the Auspices and Auguries of Birds, Octavius Retorts by Instancing the Cases of Regulus, Mancinus, Paulus, and Cæsar. And He Shows by Other Examples, that the Argument from the Oracles is of No Greater Force Than the Others.

"And now I come to those Roman auspices and auguries which you have collected with extreme pains, and have borne testimony that they were both neglected with ill consequences, and observed with good fortune. Certainly Clodius, and Flaminius, and Junius lost their armies on this account, because they did not judge it well to wait for the very solemn omen given by the greedy pecking of the chickens. But what of Regulus? Did he not observe the auguries, and was taken captive? Mancinus maintained his religious duty, and was sent under the yoke, and was given up. Paulus also had greedy chickens at Cannæ, yet he was overthrown with the greater part of the republic. Caius Cæsar despised the auguries and auspices that resisted his making his voyage into Africa before the winter, and thus the more easily he both sailed and conquered. But what and how much shall I go on to say about oracles? After his death Amphiaraus answered as to things to come, though he knew not (while living) that he should be betrayed by his wife on account of a bracelet. The blind Tiresias saw the future, although he did not see the present. Ennius invented the replies of the Pythian Apollo concerning Pyrrhus, although Apollo had already ceased to make verses; and that cautious and ambiguous oracle of his, failed just at the time when men began to be at once more cultivated and less credulous. And Demosthenes, because he knew that the answers were feigned, complained that the Pythia *philippized*. But sometimes, it is true, even auspices or oracles have touched the truth. Although among many falsehoods chance might appear as if it imitated forethought; yet I will approach the very source of error and perverseness, whence all that obscurity has flowed, and both dig into it more deeply, and lay it open more manifestly. There are some insincere and vagrant spirits degraded from their heavenly vigor by earthly stains and lusts. Now these spirits, after having lost the simplicity of their nature by being weighed down and immersed in vices, for a solace of their calamity, cease not, now that they are ruined themselves, to ruin others; and being depraved themselves, to infuse into others the error of their depravity and being themselves alienated from God, to separate others from God by the introduction of degraded superstitions. The poets know that those spirits are demons; the philosophers discourse of them; Socrates knew it, who, at the nod and decision of a demon that was at his side, either declined or undertook affairs. The Magi, also, not only know that there are demons, but, moreover, whatever miracle they affect to perform, do it by means of demons; by their aspirations and communications they show their wondrous tricks, making either those things appear which are not, or those things not to appear which are. Of those magicians, the first both in eloquence and in deed, Sosthenes, not only describes the true God with fitting majesty, but the angels that are the ministers and messengers of God, even the true God. And he knew that it enhanced His veneration, that in

The Octavius

awe of the very nod and glance of their Lord they should tremble. The same man also declared that demons were earthly, wandering, hostile to humanity. What said Plato, who believed that it was a hard thing to find out God? Does not he also, without hesitation, tell of both angels and demons? And in his *Symposium* also, does not he endeavor to explain the nature of demons? For he will have it to be a substance between mortal and immortal—that is, mediate between body and spirit, compounded by mingling of earthly weight and heavenly lightness; whence also he warns us of the desire of love, and he says that it is molded and glides into the human breast, and stirs the senses, and molds the affections, and infuses the ardor of lust.

Chapter XXVII.—Argument: Recapitulation. Doubtless Here is a Source of Error: Demons Lurk Under the Statues and Images, They Haunt the Fanes, They Animate the Fibers of the Entrails, Direct the Flights of Birds, Govern the Lots, Pour Forth Oracles Involved in False Responses. These Things Not from God; But They are Constrained to Confess When They are Adjured in the Name of the True God, and are Driven from the Possessed Bodies. Hence They Flee Hastily from the Neighborhood of Christians, and Stir Up a Hatred Against Them in the Minds of the Gentiles Who Begin to Hate Them Before They Know Them.

"These impure spirits, therefore—the demons—as is shown by the Magi, by the philosophers, and by Plato, consecrated under statues and images, lurk there, and by their afflatus attain the authority as of a present deity; while in the meantime they are breathed into the prophets, while they dwell in the shrines, while sometimes they animate the fibers of the entrails, control the flights of birds, direct the lots, are the cause of oracles involved in many falsehoods. For they are both deceived, and they deceive; inasmuch as they are both ignorant

of the simple truth, and for their own ruin they confess not that which they know. Thus they weigh men downwards from heaven, and call them away from the true God to material
things: they disturb the life, render all men unquiet; creeping also secretly into human bodies, with subtlety, as being spirits, they feign diseases, alarm the minds, wrench about the limbs; that they may constrain men to worship them, being gorged with the fumes of altars or the sacrifices of cattle, that, by remitting what they had bound, they may seem to have cured it. These raging maniacs also, whom you see rush about in public, are moreover themselves prophets without a temple; thus they rage, thus they rave, thus they are whirled around. In them also there is a like instigation of the demon, but there is a dissimilar occasion for their madness. From the same causes also arise those things which were spoken of a little time ago by you, that Jupiter demanded the restoration of his games in a dream, that the Castors appeared with horses, and that a small ship was following the leading of the matron's girdle. A great many, even some of your own people, know all those things that
the demons themselves confess concerning themselves, as often as they are driven by us from bodies by the torments of our words and by the fires of our prayers. Saturn himself,
and Serapis, and Jupiter, and whatever demons you worship, overcome by pain, speak out what they are; and assuredly they do not lie to their own discredit, especially when any of you are standing by. Since they themselves are the witnesses that they are demons, believe them when they confess the truth of themselves; for when abjured by the only and true God,
unwillingly the wretched beings shudder in their bodies, and either at once leap forth, or vanish by degrees, as the faith of the sufferer assists or the grace of the healer inspires. Thus they fly from Christians when near at hand, whom at a distance they harassed by your means in their assemblies. And thus, introduced into the minds of the ignorant, they secretly sow there a hatred of us by means of fear. For it is natural both to

The Octavius

hate one whom you fear, and to injure one whom you have feared, if you can. Thus they take possession of the minds and obstruct the hearts, that men may begin to hate us before they know us; lest, if known, they should either imitate us, or not be able to condemn us.

Chapter XXVIII.—Argument: Nor is It Only Hatred that They Arouse Against the Christians, But They Charge Against Them Horrid Crimes, Which Up to This Time Have Been Proved by Nobody. This is the Work of Demons. For by Them a False Report is Both Set on Foot and Propagated. The Christians are Falsely Accused of Sacrilege, of Incest, of Adultery, of Parricide; And, Moreover, It is Certain and True that the Very Same Crimes, or Crimes Like to or Greater Than These, are in Fact Committed by the Gentiles Themselves.

"But how unjust it is, to form a judgment on things unknown and unexamined, as you do! Believe us ourselves when penitent, for we also were the same as you, and formerly, while yet blind and obtuse, thought the same things as you; to wit, that the Christians worshipped monsters, devoured infants, mingled in incestuous banquets. And we did not perceive that such fables as these were always set afloat by those (newsmongers), and were never either inquired into nor proved; and that in so long a time no one had appeared to betray (their doings), to obtain not only pardon for their crime, but also favor for its discovery: moreover, that it was to this extent not evil, that a Christian, when accused, neither blushed nor feared, and that he only repented that he had not been one before. We, however, when we undertook to defend and protect some sacrilegious and incestuous persons, and even parricides, did not think that these (Christians) were to be heard at all. Sometimes even, when we affected to pity them, we were more cruelly violent against them, so as to torture them when they confessed, that they might deny, to wit, that they might not perish; making use of a perverse inquisition against them, not to elicit the truth, but to compel a falsehood. And if any one, by reason of greater weakness, overcome with suffering, and conquered, should deny that he was a Christian, we showed favor to him, as if by forswearing that name he had at once atoned for all his deeds by that simple denial. Do not you acknowledge that we felt and did the same as you feel and do? when, if reason and not the instigation of a demon were to judge, they should rather have been pressed not to disavow themselves Christians, but to confess themselves guilty of incests, of abominations, of sacred rites polluted, of infants immolated. For with these and such as these stories, did those same demons fill up the ears of the ignorant against us, to the horror of their execration. Nor yet was it wonderful, since the common report of men, which is, always fed by the scattering of falsehoods, is wasted away when the truth is brought to light. Thus this is the business of demons, for by them false rumors are both sown and cherished. Thence arises what you say that you hear, that an ass's head is esteemed among us a divine thing. Who is such a fool as to worship this? Who is so much more foolish as to believe that it is an object of worship? unless that you even consecrate whole asses in your stables, together with your Epona, and religiously devour those same asses with Isis. Also you offer up and worship the heads of oxen and of wethers, and you dedicate gods mingled also of a goat and a man, and gods with the faces of dogs and lions. Do you not adore and feed Apis the ox, with the Egyptians? And you do not condemn their sacred rites instituted in honor of serpents, and crocodiles, and other beasts, and birds, and fishes, of which if any one were to kill one of these gods, he is even punished with death. These same Egyptians, together with very many of you, are not more afraid of Isis than they are of the pungency of onions, nor of Serapis more than they tremble at the basest noises produced by the foulness of their bodies. He also who fables against us about our adoration of the members of the priest, tries to confer upon us what belongs really to himself. (Ista enim impudicitæ eorum forsitan sacra sint, apud quos sexus omnis membris omnibus prostat, apud quos iota impudicitia vocatur urbanitas; qui scortorum licentiæ invident, qui medios viros lambunt, libidinoso ore inguinibus inhærescunt, homines malæ linguæ etiam si tacerent, quos prius tædescit impudicitiæ suæ quam pudescit.) Abomination! they suffer on themselves such evil deeds, as no age is so effeminate as to be able to bear, and no slavery so cruel as to be compelled to endure.

Chapter XXIX.—Argument: Nor is It More True that a Man Fastened to a Cross on Account of His Crimes is Worshipped by Christians, for They Believe Not Only that He Was Innocent, But with Reason that He Was God. But, on the Other Hand, the Heathens Invoke the Divine Powers of Kings Raised into Gods by Themselves; They Pray to Images, and Beseech Their Genii.

"These, and such as these infamous things, we are not at liberty even to hear; it is even disgraceful with any more words to defend ourselves from such charges. For you pretend that those things are done by chaste and modest persons, which we should not believe to be done at all, unless you proved that they were true concerning yourselves. For in that you attribute to our religion the worship of a criminal and his cross, you wander far from the neighborhood of the truth, in thinking either that a criminal deserved, or that an earthly being was able, to be believed God. Miserable indeed is that man whose whole hope is dependent on mortal man, for all his help is put an end to with the extinction of the man. The Egyptians certainly choose out a man for themselves whom they may worship; him alone they propitiate; him they consult about all things; to him they slaughter victims; and he who to others is a god, to himself is certainly a man whether he will or no, for he does not deceive his own consciousness, if he deceives that of others. "Moreover, a false flattery disgracefully caresses princes and kings, not as great and chosen men, as is just, but as gods; whereas honor is more truly rendered to an illustrious man, and love is more pleasantly given to a very good man. Thus they invoke their deity, they supplicate their images, they implore their Genius, that is, their demon; and it is safer to swear falsely by the genius of Jupiter than by that of a king. Crosses, moreover, we neither worship nor wish for. You, indeed, who consecrate gods of wood, adore wooden crosses perhaps as parts of your gods. For your very standards, as well as your banners; and flags of your camp, what else are they but crosses glided and adorned? Your victorious trophies not only imitate the appearance of a simple cross, but also that of a man affixed to it. We assuredly see the sign of a cross, naturally, in the ship when it is carried along with swelling sails, when it glides forward with expanded oars; and when the military yoke is lifted up, it is the sign of a cross; and when a man adores God with a pure mind, with hands outstretched. Thus the sign of the cross either is sustained by a natural reason, or your own religion is formed with respect to it.

Chapter XXX.—Argument: The Story About Christians Drinking the Blood of an Infant that They Have Murdered, is a Barefaced Calumny. But the Gentiles,
Both Cruelly Expose Their Children Newly Born, and Before They are Born Destroy Them by a Cruel Abortion. Christians are Neither Allowed to See Nor to Hear of Manslaughter.

"And now I should wish to meet him who says or believes that we are initiated by the slaughter and blood of an infant. Think you that it can be possible for so tender, so little a body to receive those fatal wounds; for anyone to shed, pour forth, and drain that new blood of a youngling, and of a man scarcely come into existence? No one can believe this, except

The Octavius

one who can dare to do it. And I see that you at one time expose your begotten children to wild beasts and to birds; at another, that you crush them when strangled with a miserable kind of death. There are some women who, by drinking medical preparations, extinguish the source of the future man in their very bowels, and thus commit a parricide before they bring forth. And these things assuredly come down from the teaching of your gods. For Saturn did not expose his children, but devoured them. With reason were infants sacrificed to him by parents in some parts of Africa, caresses and kisses repressing their crying, that a weeping victim might not be sacrificed. Moreover, among the Tauri of Pontus, and to the Egyptian Busiris, it was a sacred rite to immolate their guests, and for the Galli to slaughter to Mercury human, or rather inhuman, sacrifices. The Roman sacrificers buried living a Greek man and a Greek woman, a Gallic man and a Gallic woman; and to this day, Jupiter Latiaris is worshipped by them with murder; and, what is worthy of the son of Saturn, he is gorged with the blood of an evil and criminal man. I believe that he himself taught Catiline to conspire under a compact of blood, and Bellona to steep her sacred rites with a draught of human gore, and taught men to heal epilepsy with the blood of a man, that is, with a worse disease. They also are not unlike to him who devour the wild beasts from the arena, besmeared and stained with blood, or fattened with the limbs or the entrails of men. To us it is not lawful either to see or to hear of homicide; and so much do we shrink from human blood, that we do not use the blood even of eatable animals in our food.

Chapter XXXI.—Argument: The Charge of Our Entertainments Being Polluted with Incest, is Entirely Opposed to All Probability, While It is Plain that Gentiles are Actually Guilty of Incest. The Banquets of Christians are Not Only Modest, But Temperate. In Fact, Incestuous Lust is So Unheard Of, that with Many Even the Modest Association of the Sexes Gives Rise to a Blush.

"And of the incestuous banqueting, the plotting of demons has falsely devised an enormous fable against us, to stain the glory of our modesty, by the loathing excited by an outrageous infamy, that before inquiring into the truth it might turn men away from us by the terror of an abominable charge. It was thus your own Fronto acted in this respect: he did not produce testimony, as one who alleged a charge, but he scattered reproaches as a rhetorician. For these things have rather originated from your own nations. Among the Persians, a promiscuous association between sons and mothers is allowed. Marriages with sisters are legitimate among the Egyptians and in Athens. Your records and your tragedies, which you both read and hear with pleasure, glory in incests: thus also you worship incestuous gods, who have intercourse with mothers, with daughters, with sisters. With reason, therefore, is incest frequently detected among you, and is continually permitted. Miserable men, you may even, without knowing it, rush into what is unlawful: since you scatter your lusts promiscuously, since you everywhere beget children, since you frequently expose even those who are born at home to the mercy of others, it is inevitable that you must come back to your own children, and stray to your own offspring. Thus you continue the story of incest, even although you have no consciousness of your crime. But we maintain our modesty not in appearance, but in our heart we gladly abide by the bond of a single marriage; in the desire of procreating, we know either one wife, or none at all. We practice sharing in banquets, which are not only modest, but also sober: for we do not indulge in entertainments nor prolong our feasts with wine; but we temper our joyousness with gravity, with chaste discourse, and with body even more chaste (divers of us unviolated) enjoy rather than make a boast of a perpetual virginity of a body. So far, in fact, are they from indulging in incestuous desire, that with some even the (idea of a) modest intercourse of the sexes causes a blush. Neither do we at once stand on the level of the lowest of the people, if we refuse your honors and purple robes; and we are not fastidious, if we all have a discernment of one good, but are assembled together with the same quietness with which we live as individuals; and we are not garrulous in corners, although you either blush or are afraid to hear us in public. And that day by day the number of us is increased, is not a ground for a charge of error, but is a testimony which claims praise; for, in a fair mode of life, our actual number both continues and abides undiminished, and strangers increase it. Thus, in short, we do not distinguish our people by some small bodily mark, as you suppose, but easily enough by the sign of innocence and modesty. Thus we love one another, to your regret, with a mutual love, because we do not know how to hate. Thus we call one another, to your envy, brethren: as being men born of one God and Parent, and companions in faith, and as fellow-heirs in hope. You, however, do not recognize one another, and you are cruel in your mutual hatreds; nor do you acknowledge one another as brethren, unless indeed for the purpose of fratricide.

Chapter XXXII.—Argument: Nor Can It Be Said that the Christians Conceal What They Worship Because They Have No Temples and No Altars, Inasmuch as They are Persuaded that God Can Be Circumscribed by No Temple, and that No Likeness of Him Can Be Made. But He is Everywhere Present, Sees All Things, Even the Most Secret Thoughts of Our Hearts; And We Live Near to Him, and in His Protection.

"But do you think that we conceal what we worship, if we have not temples and altars? And yet what image of God shall I make, since, if you think rightly, man himself is the image of God? What temple shall I build to Him, when this whole world fashioned by His work cannot receive Him? And when I, a man, dwell far and wide, shall I shut up the might of so great majesty within one little building? Were it not better that He should be dedicated in our mind, consecrated in our inmost heart? Shall I offer victims and sacrifices to the Lord, such as He has produced for my use, that I should throw back to Him His own gift? It is ungrateful when the victim fit for sacrifice is a good disposition, and a pure mind, and a sincere judgment. Therefore he who cultivates innocence supplicates God; he who cultivates justice makes offerings to God; he who abstains from fraudulent practices propitiates God; he who snatches man from danger slaughters the most acceptable victim. These are our sacrifices, these are our rites of God's worship; thus, among us, he who is most just is he who is most religious. But certainly the God whom we worship we neither show nor see. Verily for this reason we believe Him to be God, that we can be conscious of Him, but cannot see Him; for in His works, and in all the movements of the world, we behold His power ever present when He thunders, lightens, darts His bolts, or when He makes all bright again. Nor should you wonder if you do not see God. By the wind and by the blasts of the storm all things are driven on and shaken, are agitated, and yet neither wind nor tempest comes under our eyesight. Thus we cannot look upon the sun, which is the cause of seeing to all creatures: the pupil of the eye is withdrawn from his rays, the gaze of the beholder is dimmed; and if you look too long, all power of sight is extinguished. What! can you sustain the Architect of the sun Himself, the very source of light, when you turn yourself away from His lightnings, and hide yourself from His thunderbolts? Do you wish to see God with your carnal eyes, when you are neither able to behold nor to grasp your own soul itself, by which you are enlivened and speak? But, moreover, it is said that God is ignorant of man's doings; and being established in heaven, He can neither survey all nor know individuals. Thou errest, O man, and art deceived; for from where is God afar off, when all things heavenly and earthly, and which are beyond this province of the universe, are known to God, are full of God? Everywhere He is not only very near to us, but He is infused into us. Therefore once more look upon the sun: it is fixed fast in the heaven, yet it is diffused over all lands equally; present everywhere, it is associated and mingled with all things; its brightness is never violated. How much more God, who has made all things, and looks upon all things, from whom there can be nothing secret, is present in the darkness, is present in our thoughts, as if in the deep darkness. Not only do we act in Him, but also, I had almost said, we live with Him.

Chapter XXXIII.—Argument: That Even If God Be Said to Have Nothing Availed the Jews, Certainly the Writers of the Jewish Annals are the Most Sufficient Witnesses that They Forsook God Before They Were Forsaken by Him.

"Neither let us flatter ourselves concerning our multitude. We seem many to ourselves, but to God we are very few. We distinguish peoples and nations; to God this whole world is one family. Kings only know all the matters of their kingdom by the ministrations of their servants: God has no need of information. We not only live in His eyes, but also in His bosom. But *it is objected* that it availed the Jews nothing that they themselves worshipped the one God with altars and temples, with the greatest superstition. You are guilty of ignorance if you are recalling later events while you are forgetful or unconscious of former ones. For they themselves also, as long as they worshipped our God—and He is the same God of all—with chastity, innocence, and religion, as long as they obeyed His wholesome precepts, from a few became innumerable, from poor became rich, from being servants became kings; a few overwhelmed many; unarmed men overwhelmed armed ones as they fled from them, following them up by God's command, and with the elements striving on their behalf. Carefully read over their Scriptures, or if you are better pleased with the Roman writings, inquire concerning the Jews in the books (to say nothing of ancient documents) of Flavius Josephus or Antoninus Julianus, and you shall know that by their wickedness they deserved this fortune, and that nothing happened which had not before been predicted to them, if they should persevere in their obstinacy. Therefore you will understand that they forsook before they were forsaken, and that they were not, as you impiously say, taken captive with their God, but they were given up by God as deserters from His discipline.

Chapter XXXIV.—Argument: Moreover, It is Not at All to Be Wondered at If This World is to Be Consumed by Fire, Since Everything Which Has a Beginning Has Also an End. And the Ancient Philosophers are Not Averse from the Opinion of the Probable Burning Up of the World. Yet It is Evident that God, Having Made Man from Nothing, Can Raise Him Up from Death into Life. And All Nature Suggests a Future Resurrection.

"Further, in respect of the burning up of the world, it is a vulgar error not to believe either that fire will fall upon it in an unforeseen way, or that the world will be destroyed by it. For who of wise men doubts, who is ignorant, that all things which have had a beginning perish, all things which are made come to an end? The heaven also, with all things which are contained in heaven, will cease even as it began. The nourishment of the seas by the sweet waters of the springs shall pass away into the power of fire. The Stoics have a constant belief that, the moisture being dried up, all this world will take fire; and the Epicureans have the very same opinion concerning the conflagration of the elements and the destruction of the world. Plato speaks, saying that parts of the world are now inundated, and are now burnt up by alternate changes; and although he says that the world itself is constructed perpetual and indissoluble, yet he adds that to God Himself, the only artificer, it is both dissoluble and mortal. Thus it is no wonder if that mass be destroyed by Him by whom it was reared. You observe that philosophers dispute of the same things that we are saying, not that we are following up their tracks, but that they, from the divine announcements of the prophets, imitated the shadow of the corrupted truth. Thus also the most illustrious of the wise men, Pythagoras first, and Plato chiefly, have delivered the doctrine of resurrection with a corrupt and divided faith; for they will have it, that the bodies being dissolved, the souls alone both abide forever, and very often pass into other new bodies. To these things they add also this, by way of misrepresenting the truth, that the souls of men return into cattle, birds, and beasts. Assuredly such an opinion as that is not worthy of a philosopher's inquiry, but of the ribaldry of a buffoon. But for our argument it is sufficient, that even in this your wise men do in some measure harmonize with us. But who is so foolish or so brutish as to dare to deny that man, as he could first of all be formed by God, so can again be re-formed; that he is nothing after death, and that he was nothing before he began to exist; and as from nothing it was possible for him to be born, so from nothing it may be possible for him to be restored? Moreover, it is more difficult to begin that which is not, than to repeat that which has been. Do you think that, if anything is withdrawn from our feeble eyes, it perishes to God? Every body, whether it is dried up into dust, or is dissolved into moisture, or is compressed into ashes, or is attenuated into smoke, is withdrawn from us, but it is reserved for God in the custody of the elements. Nor, as you believe, do we fear any loss from sepulture, but we adopt the ancient and better custom of burying in the earth. See, therefore, how for our consolation all nature suggests a future resurrection. The sun sinks down and arises, the stars pass away and return, the flowers die and revive again, after their wintry decay the shrubs resume their leaves, seeds do not flourish again. Unless they are rotted: thus the body in the sepulcher is like the trees which in winter hide their verdure with a deceptive dryness. Why are you in haste for it to revive and return, while the winter is still raw? We must wait also for the spring-time of the body. And I am not ignorant that many, in the consciousness of what they deserve, rather desire than believe that they shall be nothing after death; for they would prefer to be altogether extinguished, rather than to be restored for the purpose of punishment. And their error also is enhanced, both by the liberty granted them in this life, and by

God's very great patience, whose judgment, the more tardy it is, is so much the more just.

Chapter XXXV.—Argument: Righteous and Pious Men Shall Be Rewarded with Never-Ending Felicity, But Unrighteous Men Shall Be Visited with Eternal Punishment. The Morals of Christians are Far More Holy Than Those of the Gentiles.

"And yet men are admonished in the books and poems of the most learned poets of that fiery river, and of the heat flowing in manifold turns from the Stygian marsh,—things which, prepared for eternal torments, and known to them by the information of demons and from the oracles of their prophets, they have delivered to us. And therefore among them also even king Jupiter himself swears religiously by the parching banks and the black abyss; for, with foreknowledge of the punishment destined to him, with his worshippers, he shudders. Nor is there either measure or termination to these torments. There the intelligent fire burns the limbs and restores them, feeds on them and nourishes them. As the fires of the thunderbolts strike upon the bodies, and do not consume them; as the fires of Mount Ætna and of Mount Vesuvius, and of burning lands everywhere, glow, but are not wasted; so that penal fire is not fed by the waste of those who burn, but is nourished by the unexhausted eating away of their bodies. But that they who know not God are deservedly tormented as impious, as unrighteous persons, no one except a profane man hesitates to believe, since it is not less wicked to be ignorant of, than to offend the Parent of all, and the Lord of all. And although ignorance of God is sufficient for punishment, even as knowledge of Him is of avail for pardon, yet if we Christians be compared with you, although in some things our discipline is inferior, yet we shall be found much better than you. For you forbid, and yet commit, adulteries; we are born *men* only for our own wives: you punish crimes when committed; with us, even to think of crimes is to sin: you are afraid of those who are aware of what you do; we are even afraid of our own conscience alone, without which we cannot exist: finally, from your numbers the prison boils over; but there is no Christian there, unless he is accused on account of his religion, or a deserter.

Chapter XXXVI.—Argument: Fate is Nothing, Except So Far as Fate is God. Man's Mind is Free, and Therefore So is His Action: His Birth is Not Brought into Judgment. It is Not a Matter of Infamy, But of Glory, that Christians are Reproached for Their Poverty; And the Fact that They Suffer Bodily Evils is Not as a Penalty, But as a Discipline.

"Neither let anyone either take comfort from, or apologize for what happens from fate. Let what happens be of the disposition of fortune, yet the mind is free; and therefore man's doing, not his dignity, is judged. For what else is fate than what God has spoken of each one of us? who, since He can foresee our constitution, determines also the fates for us, according to the deserts and the qualities of individuals. Thus in our case it is not the star under which we are born that is punished, but the particular nature of our disposition is blamed. And about fate enough is said; or if, in consideration of the time, we have spoken too little, we shall argue the matter at another time more abundantly and more fully. But that many of us are called poor, this is not our disgrace, but our glory; for as our mind is relaxed by luxury, so it is strengthened by frugality. And yet who can be poor if he does not want, if he does not crave for the possessions of others, if he is rich towards God? He rather is poor, who, although he has much, desires more. Yet I will speak according as I feel. No one can be so poor as he is born. Birds live without any patrimony, and day by day the cattle are fed; and yet these creatures are born

The Octavius

for us—all of which things, if we do not lust after, we possess. Therefore, as he who treads a road is the happier the lighter he walks, so happier is he in this journey of life who lifts himself along in poverty, and does not breathe heavily under the burden of riches. And yet even if we thought wealth useful to us, we should ask it of God. Assuredly He might be able to indulge us in some measure, whose is the whole; but we would rather despise riches than possess them: we desire rather innocence, we rather entreat for patience, we prefer being good to being prodigal; and that we feel and suffer the human mischiefs of the body is not punishment—it is warfare. For fortitude is strengthened by infirmities, and calamity is very often the discipline of virtue; in addition, strength both of mind and of body grows torpid without the exercise of labor. Therefore all your mighty men whom you announce as an example have flourished illustriously by their afflictions. And thus God is neither unable to aid us, nor does He despise us, since He is both the ruler of all men and the lover of His own people. But in adversity He looks into and searches out each one; He weighs the disposition of every individual in dangers, even to death at last; He investigates the will of man, certain that to Him nothing can perish. Therefore, as gold by the fires, so are we declared by critical moments.

Chapter XXXVII.—Argument: Tortures Most Unjustly Inflicted for the Confession of Christ's Name are Spectacles Worthy of God. A Comparison Instituted Between Some of the Bravest of the Heathens and the Holy Martyrs. He Declares that Christians Do Not Present Themselves at Public Shows and Processions, Because They Know Them, with the Greatest Certainty, to Be No Less Impious Than Cruel.

"How beautiful is the spectacle to God when a Christian does battle with pain; when he is drawn up against threats, and punishments, and tortures; when, mocking the noise of death, he treads underfoot the horror of the executioner; when he raises up his liberty against kings and princes, and yields to God alone, whose he is; when, triumphant and victorious, he tramples upon the very man who has pronounced sentence against him! For he has conquered who has obtained that for which he contends. What soldier would not provoke peril with greater boldness under the eyes of his general? For no one receives a reward before his trial, and yet the general does not give what he has not: he cannot preserve life, but he can make the warfare glorious. But God's soldier is neither forsaken in suffering, nor is brought to an end by death. Thus the Christian may seem to be miserable; he cannot be really found to be so. You yourselves extol unfortunate men to the skies; Mucius Scævola, for instance, who, when he had failed in his attempt against the king, would have perished among the enemies unless he had sacrificed his right hand. And how many of our people have borne that not their right hand only, but their whole body, should be burned— burned up without any cries of pain, especially when they had it in their power to be sent away! Do I compare men with Mucius or Aquilius, or with Regulus? Yet boys and young women among us treat with contempt crosses and tortures, wild beasts, and all the bugbears of punishments, with the inspired patience of suffering. And do you not perceive, O wretched men, that there is nobody who either is willing without reason to undergo punishment, or is able without God to bear tortures? Unless, perhaps, the fact has deceived you, that those who know not God abound in riches, flourish in honors, and excel in power. Miserable men! in this respect they are lifted up the higher, that they may fall down lower. For these are fattened as victims for punishment, as sacrifices they are crowned for the slaughter. Thus in this respect some are lifted up to empires and dominations, that the unrestrained exercise of power might make a market of their spirit to the unbridled license that is characteristic of a ruined soul. For, apart from the knowledge of God, what solid happiness can there be, since death must

The Octavius

come? Like a dream, happiness slips away before it is grasped. Are you a king? Yet you fear as much as you are feared; and however you may be surrounded with abundant followers, yet you are alone in the presence of danger. Are you rich? But fortune is ill trusted; and with a large travelling equipage the brief journey of life is not furnished, but burdened. Do you boast of the fasces and the magisterial robes? It is a vain mistake of man, and an empty worship of dignity, to glitter in purple and to be sordid in mind. Are you elevated by nobility of birth? do you praise your parents? Yet we are all born with one lot; it is only by virtue that we are distinguished. We therefore, who are estimated by our character and our modesty, reasonably abstain from evil pleasures, and from your pomp and exhibitions, the origin of which in connection with sacred things we know, and condemn their mischievous enticements. For in the chariot games who does not shudder at the madness of the people brawling among themselves? or at the teaching of murder in the gladiatorial games? In the scenic games also the madness is not less, but the debauchery is more prolonged: for now a mimic either expounds or shows forth adulteries; now nerveless player, while he feigns lust, suggests it; the same actor disgraces your gods by attributing to them adulteries, sighs, hatreds; the same provokes your tears with pretended sufferings, with vain gestures and expressions. Thus you demand murder, in fact, while you weep at it in fiction.

Chapter XXXVIII.—Argument: Christians Abstain from Things Connected with Idol Sacrifices, Lest Any One Should Think Either that They Yield to Demons, or that They are Ashamed of Their Religion. They Do Not Indeed Despise All the Color and Scent of Flowers, for They are Accustomed to Use Them Scattered About Loosely and Negligently, as Well as to Entwine Their Necks with Garlands; But to Crown the Head of a Corpse They Think Superfluous and Useless. Moreover, with the Same Tranquility with Which They Live They Bury Their Dead, Waiting with a Very Certain Hope the Crown of Eternal Felicity. Therefore Their Religion, Rejecting All the Superstitions of the Gentiles, Should Be Adopted as True by All Men.

"But that we despise the leavings of sacrifices, and the cups out of which libations have been poured, is not a confession of fear, but an assertion of our true liberty. For although nothing which comes into existence as an inviolable gift of God is corrupted by any agency, yet we abstain, lest any should think either that we are submitting to demons, to whom libation has been made, or that we are ashamed of our religion. But who is he who doubts of our indulging ourselves in spring flowers, when we gather both the rose of spring and the lily, and whatever else is of agreeable color and odour among the flowers? For these we both use scattered loose and free, and we twine our necks with them in garlands. Pardon us, forsooth, that we do not crown our heads; we are accustomed to receive the scent of a sweet flower in our nostrils, not to inhale it with the back of our head or with our hair. Nor do we crown the dead. And in this respect I the more wonder at you, in the way in which you apply to a lifeless person, or to one who does not feel, a torch; or a garland to one who does not smell it, when either as blessed he does not want, or, being miserable, he has no pleasure in, flowers. Still we adorn our obsequies with the

same tranquility with which we live; and we do not bind to us a withering garland, but we wear one living with eternal
flowers from God, since we, being both moderate and secure in the liberality of our God, are animated to the hope of future felicity by the confidence of His present majesty. Thus
we both rise again in blessedness, and are already living in contemplation of the future. Then let Socrates the Athenian buffoon see to it, confessing that he knew nothing, although
boastful in the testimony of a most deceitful demon; let Arcesilaus also, and Carneades, and Pyrrho, and all the multitude of the Academic philosophers, deliberate; let Simonides also for ever put off the decision of his opinion. We despise the bent brows of the philosophers, whom we know to be corrupters, and adulterers, and tyrants, and ever eloquent against their own vices. We who bear wisdom not in our dress, but in our mind, we do not speak great things, but we live them; we boast that we have attained what they have sought
for with the utmost eagerness, and have not been able to find. Why are we ungrateful? Why do we grudge if the truth of divinity has ripened in the age of our time? Let us enjoy our
benefits, and let us in rectitude moderate our judgments; let superstition be restrained; let impiety be expiated; let true religion be preserved.

Chapter XXXIX.—Argument: When Octavius Had Finished This Address, Minucius and Cæcilius Sate for Some Time in Attentive and Silent Wonder. And Minucius Indeed Kept Silence in Admiration of Octavius, Silently Revolving What He Had Heard.

When Octavius had brought his speech to a close, for some time we were struck into silence, and held our countenances fixed in attention and as for me, I was lost in the greatness of my admiration, that he had so adorned those things which it is easier to feel than to say, both by arguments and by examples, and by authorities derived from reading; and that he had repelled the malevolent objectors with the very weapons of the philosophers with which they are armed, and had moreover shown the truth not only as easy, but also as agreeable.

Chapter XL.—Argument: Then Cæcilius Exclaims that He is Vanquished by Octavius; And That, Being Now Conqueror Over Error, He Professes the Christian Religion. He Postpones, However, Till the Morrow His Training in the Fuller Belief of Its Mysteries.

While, therefore, I was silently turning over these things in my own mind, Cæcilius broke forth: "I congratulate as well my Octavius as myself, as much as possible on that tranquility in which we live, and I do not wait for the decision. Even thus we have conquered: not unjustly do I assume to myself the victory. For even as he is my conqueror, so I am triumphant over error. Therefore, in what belongs to the substance of the question, I both confess concerning providence, and I yield to God; and I agree concerning the sincerity of the way of life which is now mine. Yet even still some things remain in my mind, not as resisting the truth, but as necessary to a perfect training of which on the morrow, as the sun is already sloping to his setting, we shall inquire at length in a more fitting and ready manner."

Chapter XLI.—Argument: Finally, All are Pleased, and Joyfully Depart: Cæcilius, that He Had Believed; Octavius, that He Had Conquered; And Minucius, that the Former Had Believed, and the Latter Had Conquered.

"But for myself," said I, "I rejoice more fully on behalf of all of us; because also Octavius has conquered for me, in that the very great invidiousness of judging is taken away from me. Nor can I acknowledge by my praises the merit of his words: the testimony both of man, and of one man only, is weak. He has an illustrious reward from God, inspired by

The Octavius

whom he has pleaded, and aided by whom he has gained the victory." After these things we departed, glad and cheerful: Cæcilius, to rejoice that he had believed; Octavius, that he had succeeded; and I, that the one had believed, and the other had conquered.

Elucidations.

I.

(Editions, p. 171.)

For an interesting account of the bibliographical history of this work, see Dupin. It passed for the Eight Book of Arnobius until a.d. 1560, and was first printed in its true character at Heidelberg in that year, with a learned preface by Balduinus, who restored it to its true author.

II.

(The neighing of horses, note 1, p. 183.)

It strikes me as singular that the Edinburgh edition, which gives a note to each of the instances that follow, should have left me to supply this reference to the case of Darius Hystaspes. The story is told, as will be remembered by all who have ever read it, by Herodotus, and is certainly one of the most extraordinary in history, when one reflects that a horse elected a great monarch, and one whose life not a little affected the fortunes of mankind. A knavish groom was indeed the engineer of this election, as often, in such events, the secret springs of history are hidden; but, if the story is not wholly a fable, the coincidence of thunder in the heavens is most noteworthy. It seemed to signify the overruling of Providence, and the power of God to turn the folly, not less than the wrath, of men, to God's praise. See Herod., book iii. cap. lxxxvi.

III.

(From nothing, p. 194.)

From this chapter, if not from others, it had been rashly affirmed that our author imagined that the soul perishes with the body, and is to be renewed out of nothing. The argument is wholly *ad hominem*, and asserts nothing from the author's own point of view, as I understand it. He gives what is "sufficient for his argument," and professes nothing more. He was not a clergyman, nor is his work a sermon to the faithful. He defies any one to deny, that, if God could form man out of nothing, He can make him anew out of nothing. The residue of the argument is a brilliant assertion of the imperishability of matter, in terms which might satisfy modern science; and the implication is, that the soul no more perishes to the sight of God than does the body vaporized and reserved in the custody of the elements.

www.ingramcontent.com/pod-product-compliance
Ingram Content Group UK Ltd.
Pitfield, Milton Keynes, MK11 3LW, UK
UKHW021315141225
9555UKWH00032B/541